Toronto's Lost Villages

D1242691

Toronto's Lost Villages

Ron Brown

Polar Bear Press
Toronto

TORONTO'S LOST VILLAGES. © 1997 by Ron Brown. All rights reserved. No part of this book may be used or reproduced in any manner whatsoever without prior written permission except in the case of brief quotations embodied in reviews. For information, contact Polar Bear Press, 35 Prince Andrew Place, Toronto, Ontario M3C 2H2

First edition

distributed by
North 49 Books
35 Prince Andrew Place
Toronto, Ontario M3C 2H2
(416) 449-4000

Canadian Cataloguing in Publication Data

Brown, Ron, 1945-
      Toronto's Lost Villages

Includes bibliographical references and index.
ISBN 1-896757-02-2

1.   Historic sites – Ontario – Toronto Region
2.   Toronto Region (Ont.) – History. I. Title

FC3097.43B76 1997   971.3'54   C97-930551-9
F1059.5.T6857B76 1997

Printed in Canada

Table of Contents

Introduction

We can all notice, as we get a little older, the difference that even five years can make to the face of a city. Storefronts change, buildings disappear, new structures are erected seemingly overnight.

And in ten years? In ten years entire streets, sometimes even entire neighbourhoods can be altered to the point where they become virtually unrecognizable to us as we visit our old haunts. The older a city gets, the newer it seems to look.

Now try to imagine what Toronto might have looked like not five or ten years back, but 200 years. It was about then, in 1793, to be exact, that Colonel John Graves Simcoe pulled into the modest harbour, on the north shore of Lake Ontario opposite Newark, the capital (now Niagara-on-the-Lake). The closest viable British settlement was Kingston, too far to the east to be of much help to the capital should the Yankees decide to attack.

So it was here, beside a swamp surrounded by nearly impenetrable wilderness, that Simcoe ordered the settlement built. In the four years that he remained at the colony, he accomplished a great deal in the way of political infrastructure, but the little settlement of York would have to wait still many years before it would achieve much of anything. Even by 1810, York could claim only a few hundred settlers.

How do you suppose Simcoe might react if we could bring him into our timeline, and show him what has become of his little settlement by the swamp; and of the dozens of hamlets, mill towns and whistlestops that sprang up around it.

In essence, this is what Toronto's Lost Villages is all about: the time in between then and now; the enormous, unfathomable changes that time has wrought; the people who struggled to settle in a rough land, and the settlements they built. Where are these places now? Are they gone forever, buried under years and asphalt? Are some of them still here but only forgotten — an old mill chimney beside a farmer's field, a rustic colonial home trapped between a busy street and a highrise, between a forgotten past and an uncertain future?

If you are the slightest bit curious about where your city or town came from, or whether any evidence at all of those pioneer days still lingers on our city streets or beside our roaring highways, then I advise you to read on. A great adventure awaits.

Ron Brown
May, 1997

Map One

Ports, Pioneer Paths, Lost Villages of Yonge Street, Dundas Street and Kingston Road

CLAIRVILLE

SMITHFIELD

St. ANDREWS

Yonge Street

LAMBTON   CARLTON

ISLINGTON   DAVENPORT

DRUMMONDVILLE

BROCKTON

SUMMERVILLE   Str.   YORKVILLE

DIXIE   Dundas   WINDERMERE   BLUE   NEW
                                   BELL   TOWN

COOKSVILLE   HUMBER BAY

SPRINGFIELD   LONG BRANCH

LORNE PARK   L a k e

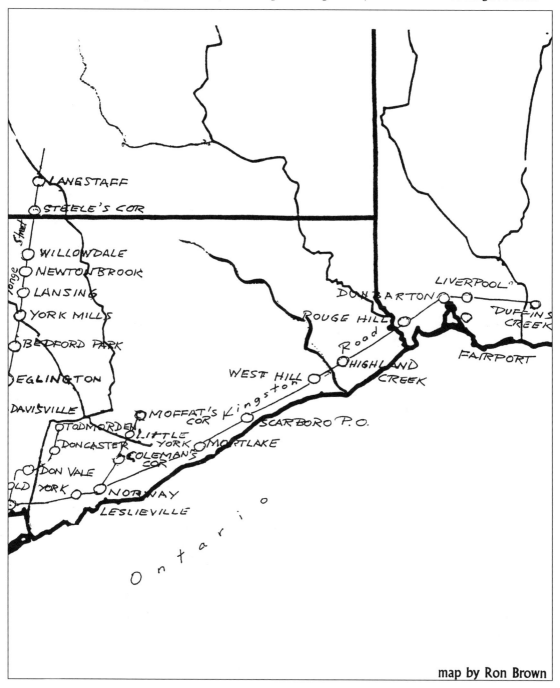

map by Ron Brown

Windermere

1.

Along the Lakeshore

T he year was 1793, and the shore of Lake Ontario was still thick with forests. The few clearings were hazy with the smoke of Indian campfires, while ducks flapped across the little lagoons that hid in the frequent river mouths. Crumbling ruins marked the scattered sites of early forts and fur posts. Well-worn foot trails and portages wound through the dark woods, linking the all-important rivers and lakes which, to the inhabitants of the day, were their highways.

Those water routes were as important to the lakeshore's first non-native settlers as they were to the aboriginal inhabitants. Eastern Ontario and the Niagara Peninsula already had a few crude villages ringing the little harbours, and with the arrival of John Graves Simcoe in 1793, development would soon spread to the area which, 200 years later, would become the seemingly endless urban sprawl known as Toronto.

Old York

This, the oldest of Toronto's "lost villages," has undergone many transformations. From a cluster of wooden huts in a dark forest clearing in the 1790s, York, as it was first called, had evolved by the 1830s into a handsome, if muddy, provincial town of banks, churches and stores. But in 1853 the railways began to transform what is now called Toronto into a smoky, industrial city. The majority of those industries, in turn, have disappeared, replaced now by condos, town houses and soaring glass skyscrapers.

The enormity of the changes belies the scant time in which they have occurred. 1793, after all, is just a little over 200 years ago. Yet it was in July of that year that John Graves Simcoe, commander of the Queens Rangers, landed in the schooner Mississauga on the low shores, to a silent woodland. His job was to find and lay out a new capital for Britain's new province of Upper Canada. The existing capital, Newark (now Niagara-on-the-Lake), was too exposed to the Americans with whom Britain had just fought the War of Independence. With Simcoe were chief surveyor Augustus Jones, and his deputy, Alexander Aitken, whose task was to find a place to put a new town.

Rather than choose the grounds around the old French fort near the foot of today's Dufferin Street, as proposed in a plan prepared by Captain Gotherman, a British army surveyor, five years earlier, they chose instead the head of the swampy harbour where a creek known as the Don River flowed into the bay. Here they laid out ten square blocks; five along the shore and two deep.

In August, then Governor Simcoe named the new town York, after Frederick, Duke of York, the son of King George III. The Township that surrounded it was called Dublin. The following year, Simcoe began the construction of the new parlia-

Berkeley Castle's ignominious final years before its demolition.

12

When first con-structed, Berkeley Castle was one of York's grandest homes.

ment buildings, located at today's Front and Berkeley Streets, then known as Parliament and Palace.

By 1810, York had grown to about 600 inhabitants, most of them related to the government of the province. These included the legislators, their bureaucrats, the military, and the merchants that served them. There were also a half dozen stores, a like number of hotels, but only a solitary church. The only industries were those serving the needs of the inhabitants: a brewery, a distillery, a potashery, a bakery and a slaughterhouse. Thomas Skinner's grist mill stood on the Don River a good distance northeast, while the Kingsmill stood on the Humber to the west. On the streets huddled about a hundred houses. The forest around them remained largely still and dark, for pioneers had only begun to hack down the huge trees. A rivulet named Taddle Creek cut across the top of the village to join the Don River near its mouth. The harbour was marshy and ringed with trees, while a forested sand spit stabbed out into the lake. The isolation of the tiny capital was palpable, and daunting to the settlers.

Those who braved the potholed trails that passed for roads could follow the Kingston Road east, Dundas Street or the

Lakeshore Road west, or Yonge Street north. To reach Kingston Road, travellers had to follow what is today King Street across the long-lost Taddle Creek, before reaching Kingston Road at a point where King now joins Queen. Although it was the base line for the concession roads being laid out further north, Queen Street, or "Lot", as it was then known, was not a through road, as it was cut off by the creek.

To reach Dundas Street, travellers had to follow Adelaide Street from the corner of New Street (Jarvis), and along Queen Street to today's Ossington, which was the beginning of Dundas.

As early as 1837, Old York was beginning to disappear. New Street stretched west to Simcoe Street, while Yonge Street was extended to the lake. King Street was fast becoming the fashionable new main street, as the town centre developed around New Street and King. Here stood the new town hall, jail, customs house and the beautiful St. James Anglican Church. Industries had begun to appear as well, with Enoch Turner's Brewery and the James Gooderham Distillery, and a flourishing farmers' market behind the town hall. A new Bank of Upper Canada and a handsome post office had opened up side by side on the northeast corner of Duke and George. In those days, the corner of Yonge and Queen, considered the commercial centre of the City now, had only a tannery and a foundry, and was considered "out of town."

Naming of Yonge Street

Named by Simcoe in honor of his friend, British Secretary of War, Sir George Yonge.

Gone too were most of the huts of log and lumber, replaced by appropriately grand mansions to befit the evolving bourgeoisie. Among these were the Campbell House on the northwest corner of Duke and Caroline (today's Adelaide and Sherbourne), a neoclassical brick building built in 1825, the Ridout House at Duke and Princess, the three-storey Arnold House near George and Duchess (Richmond), the sprawling Widmer House at Ontario and Palace (Front), and the Berkeley "Castle", a thirteen-room English manor, with yard and garden, sitting grandly on one acre of land at the southwest corner of King and Berkeley.

14

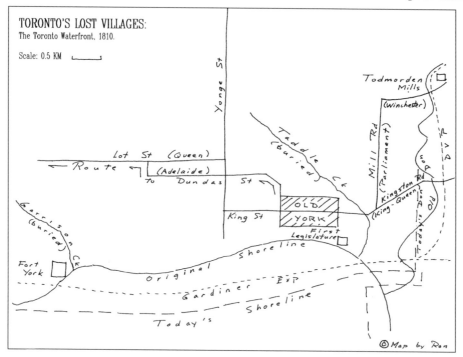

TORONTO'S LOST VILLAGES:
The Toronto Waterfront, 1810.

Scale: 0.5 KM

© Map by Ron

The parliament buildings, meanwhile, had gone from their early location on Front, burned by American soldiers in 1813, and again a mere decade later, due to a defective flue. The new site was a six-acre plot bounded by today's Front, Wellington, John and Peter Streets.

But the biggest transformations occurred between the 1850s and the 1880s. This marked the arrival of the Railway Era, and the most dramatic changes Toronto would experience along its lakeshore. Although early city councils were opposed to the placing of the railways along a shoreline that was supposed to remain open and public, the influence of the private sector, as usual, won the day. Rail yards, wharves and factories filled in the shoreline, which itself was obliterated by numerous landfill efforts. The new uses pushed out the houses and the fine stores, and Old York became Toronto's industrial centre. With the arrival of the post war car craze, Lakeshore Boulevard was widened to six lanes, while the unfortunately-situated and ele-

York's fourth post office on Adelaide Street is now a post office museum.

vated Gardiner Expressway completed the barricading of the lake from the city.

Throughout the 1960s another transformation would occur. With the blooming of the suburbs, the old rail-oriented industries became obsolete. Nearly all have closed, replaced now with townhouses, and condominiums, or renovated into theatres or offices. Few buildings remain which date from the days of "Old" or pre-1837, York.

The grand homes of the Widmers, the Ridouts and the Arnolds are long gone. Only the Campbell House survives now in a new location, as a lawyers' club at the northwest corner of University and Queen. Perhaps the best example of heritage preservation in the Toronto area is the restoration of the Bank of Upper Canada and the post office. Built in 1827, the three-storey stone bank building at the northeast corner of Duke and George was only the second used by the first chartered bank in Upper Canada. Its two upper floors housed Thomas Ridout, the first general manager. Next door stood York's fourth post office. Built on land purchased from the bank for 500 pounds sterling and originally the house of James Scott Howard, it was designed to complement the grandeur of the bank. Howard operated York's fourth post office in it from 1834 until 1838. Employing six people, he stayed open from eight a.m. to seven p.m., Monday to Saturday, and nine to ten a.m. on Sunday. Howard was dismissed as postmaster in 1838 following the aborted rebellion of the previous year.

During the interim, the De LaSalle Catholic School was built between the two old buildings. Since then the buildings gradually deteriorated, used ignominiously as a biscuit factory, for egg storage, and as an armed forces recruitment centre. By

16

1978, they sat abandoned and following a fire were slated for demolition. However, a visionary and heritage lover, Sheldon Godfrey, rescued them from demolition and restored them, an accomplishment that earned him architectural achievement awards as well as awards from the Ontario Historical Society and the Ministry of Citizenship and Culture. The old bank and school now house offices, while the post office is a fully functioning post-office museum.

Elsewhere, a trio of King Street's early stores, built during the 1830s, still stands at the northeast corner of King and Jarvis, while at the southeast corner of King and George, (187 King), stands what was the Little York Hotel, an 1880s replacement for one of Old York's most popular hostelries.

Throughout this much changed area, a number of buildings date from the 1840-1860 period, when Old York was becoming just a memory for early Torontonians. These include the magnificent Gooderham and Worts Distillery, now undergoing restoration, a portion of which dates from 1859. At King and Trinity, a couple of blocks east of Old York, the Little Trinity Church (1843) and the Enoch Turner Schoolhouse (1848), Ontario's first "public" school, are both preserved. Close by, at

Industries like Gooderham & Worts – this structure built in 1859 – mark the end of Old York as a village

17

the southeast corner of King and Parliament stands what is left of an early Kingston Road Hotel, the Derby, built in 1846. At the corner of King and Berkeley, (298-300 King), a pair of houses built by Charles Small, son of Major John Small who owned the Berkeley Castle, date from 1845. The building at 302 King was once the Garibaldi House, an early wayside tavern built in 1859.

And of the old Parliament Buildings, their existence is commemorated in the name of a small uninteresting park at the foot of Berkeley Street, called simply Parliament Square.

New Town

By 1800, Simcoe had returned to England (where he died soon after), and his successor, Peter Russell, was anxious to place his own distinct imprint upon the layout of the new capital. As

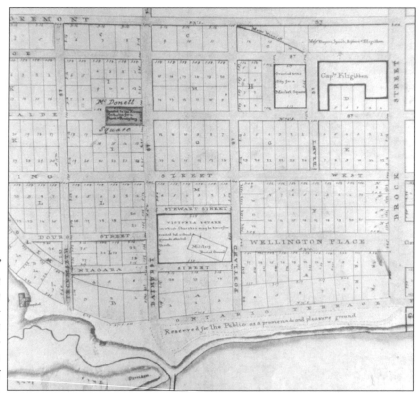

"New Town" was an early effort to apply Washington-style parks and boulevards to an expanding urban fringe.

18

Victoria Memorial Park and Clarence Square anchored the proposed grand boulevard to be called "Wellington Place". This is the view from Victoria Park.

Simcoe had done east of Yonge Street, Russell laid out an extension west of it stretching south of Lot Street between Yonge and Peter. The lots here were considerably larger than those in Old York, each being larger than six lots in the old town. Special lots were set aside for the more important buildings such as the parliament buildings, and government house. The new centre of town was the area around today's King and Simcoe. Upper Canada College stood north of King from 1829 to 1900, as did Government House, the lieutenant governor's residence, between King and Wellington, and the parliament buildings themselves between Wellington and Front.

West of this extension, Toronto's first effort at urban design was the area called New Town. The original concept for New Town, designed in 1833 by Deputy Surveyor H.J. Castle, was based on a circle, at what is today the intersection of Bathurst and King. But the plan was revised and the focus instead shift-

19

A row of historic houses on Draper Street are surrounded by the factories and warehouses that invaded "New Town"

ed to a Washington- style plan with two town squares, Clarence Square and Victoria Square, linked by a grand treed boulevard called Wellington Place. Bounded by Peter Street on the east, New Town stretched west to Garrison Creek, a now vanished rivulet indicated today only by the curving pattern of Niagara Street. The largest lots lined the lakefront on the north side of Front Street across which was a strip of land used "for a public pleasure ground" (which, if used for anything else, would revert to the crown). Bathurst Street itself extended to Front Street where a government ordinance wharf was located.

While several of Toronto's more prominent families took up the spacious lots (like the Anglican bishop, the receiver general and the chief justice), New Town remained for the most part only lightly developed.

As in Old York, the arrival of the railways changed the face of New Town utterly. The noise and the smoke of the steam engines and the factories they attracted soon chased away the fledgling aristocracy. The Grand Trunk and the Toronto and Hamilton (Great Western) Railways both coveted the shoreline for its access to shipping. By 1858 the lake had been filled in and wharves lined the shore from the fort to the market. Old York and New Town had been severed from their waterfront roots, a planning miscalculation which was later compounded by more wharves, more rail lines, and ultimately, the ill-conceived elevated Gardiner Expressway.

The grand town lots soon filled with factories and warehouses; a landscape that in a century has changed little. However, there is evidence still of this early effort at grand urban design.

*Clarence Square
marked the east end
of New Town's
"Wellington Place".*

Both Clarence Square and Victoria Square still survive, while between the two, Wellington Street has retained its boulevard appearance, with trees lining the roadway, and the factories and warehouses set well back from the street. The vista remains elegant as well, each of the squares easily visible from each other, as the original design intended. The war memorial in the centre of Victoria Square contains two dozen headstones from New Town's first days, although weather and pollution have made most of them unreadable. Clarence Square remained undeveloped until the late 19th century when a row of elegant townhouses were built along the north side, an aspect which makes the site highly sought by film crews.

Finding original buildings, however, is a little harder. Although most disappeared with the wave of industrialization, a few yet linger. Number 24 Mercer Street represents the 1859 house of well-known lawyer John Reed, and was designed by his neighbour, prominent architect John Tully. Early workers' houses line Draper Street between Wellington and Front, most sporting plaques proclaiming them to heritage homes. Homes at the northeast corner of Wellington and Portland, and at 422 Wellington represent the last vestiges of Wellington Place's attempts to be an urban boulevard.

East of Clarence Square, the double houses at 50 - 52 Peter Street were built by Receiver General George Crookshank, who owned an estate property to the south of them. With the decline of the neighbourhood, the buildings were used as boarding houses, warehousing, and an agency for destitute children. Unfortunately, subsequent renovations largely obliterated the original appearance of these once attractive early houses.

Near the fringe of New Town, Joseph Bishop, a local butcher, in 1833 built a row of five houses for speculative purposes. Two still stand and can be found at 192-194 Adelaide Street West. However, the most prominent symbol of the attempt at a grand new town is found in one of Toronto's finest buildings, Osgoode Hall. When first built in 1832, it stood majestically at the head of a country lane now called York Street. Designed by John Ewart, the original hall, named after the first justice of the peace, William Osgoode, consisted only of what is today's east wing. The centre block and west wing were added in 1844, and the famous cattle gates in 1866. The magnificent structure is a welcome relief amid the architectural tedium that now dominates University Avenue.

The removal of the railway yards in the 1970s - 1980s changed the face of the area once more, with the arrival of the CN Tower, the Metro Convention Centre, and the new CBC building, while the side streets grew into Toronto's newest Night Club district.

Windermere

Lakeshore Road, one of the west Toronto area's busiest roads, is also one of its oldest. Some have maintained that Lakeshore Road predates even Yonge Street. Certainly it seems that Governor Simcoe's surveyor, Augustus Jones, was working on it in 1791, two years before Simcoe's arrival, and five years before Yonge Street's conception. Prior to that it was an Indian trail along the shore of the lake.

But even as late as 1812, there were no bridges over the main rivers, travellers having to use the several toll ferries. Along the road, taverns sprang up to provide rest and refreshment to the bone-weary wayfarers, while wharves were opened to ship out grain, lumber and other pioneer produce.

In 1853, the Toronto and Hamilton Railway laid its tracks beside the lake and boosted the economies of the communities lucky enough to rate a station. Then in 1917, the Lakeshore Road was paved and renamed the Hamilton Highway. In 1939, Queen Elizabeth, now the Queen Mother, opened North America's first limited access highway, the Queen Elizabeth Way, beating out the Pennsylvania Turnpike by a year.

The Lakeshore Road

An early native trail along the lake, the route became Canada's first concrete highway when the Toronto Hamilton Highway was opened in 1917.

At each stanza in the lakeshore's transportation saga, old villages were swallowed up and vanished. Windermere was one of those. Long lost in the story of Toronto's growth, it was located on Humber Bay between Grenadier Pond and the mouth of the Humber River. As a small village it contained a church, general store, bolt works and a handful of workers' houses while a small board-and-batten railway station served the community. The church, St. Olaves by the Lake, was built in 1886 on land donated by the Ontario Bolt Company. Started after the arrival of the railways, the Bolt company was located at the foot of Windermere Avenue, and by 1885 employed 200 workers.It was the largest such plant west of Toronto. A short distance east were the Ontario Rolling Mill Company and the Grenadier Ice Company, which began operation in 1880, adding icehouses and employing 18 workers.

But the little lakeside village would soon fall to the suburban boom that was sweeping outward from Toronto. The Bolt Company owned 200 acres of land stretching back up the hill towards Bloor Street. With the extension of streetcar service along Bloor, and speculation that the College Street service would be extended through High Park (which did not happen), the company subdivided the land between what is today Morningside Road (but then called College Street) and Bloor. In 1889 Windermere became the attractive hillside suburb of Swansea.

With the paving and widening of Lakeshore Road, and with the building of the Queen Elizabeth Way, all traces of old Windermere have vanished. The only evidence that there even was a place by that name is Swansea's main thoroughfare, Windermere Avenue, which leads to the site of the one-time lakeside village. St. Olave's Road is all that is left of the old church, while Ellis Avenue now marks the location of the Rolling Mills. Swansea's era as a separate municipality ended in 1967, but the community lives on.

Humber Bay

A short distance west of Windermere, the protection offered by the mouth of the Humber River, and the presence of a toll ferry across it, provided the impetus for the development of the little port of Humber Bay.

In 1803, ferryman Donald Cameron was charging travellers six cents each, or sixteen cents for their carriage and horses. He was succeeded in 1815 by another Scotsman named McLean, who converted his dwelling into a pub, then the only stopping place between York and the Credit River. Humber Bay is on its way to becoming one of the more popular watering spots west of Toronto. After McLean perished in a snowstorm in 1834, his widow, "Mother" McLean operated the tavern until her death at 94. The weathered old pub, however, stood in the path of the Great Western Railway, and was demolished.The demise of the wharf did not mean the end of the port. Because of the many bad stretches along Dundas Street further inland, Lakeshore Road gradually became the busier of the two. Even with the replacement of the ferry with a crude log bridge in 1824, Humber Bay remained a notorious collection of taverns and inns. Devins restaurant with dance hall on the second floor became a popular destination for York's sporting crowd. John McDowell added a tavern in 1852, with three more appearing in the 1860s and 70s.

The Royal Oak was noted for the tree growing through its verandah, a well-equipped reading room and popular banquet hall. Charles Nurse operated a hotel along with his boatworks.

Today's Lakeshore Boulevard is a far cry from when it was a pioneer path skirting Humber Bay.

Beside it he added a fishpond and bicycle path. But likely the best known of the lot was John Duck's tavern. Located to the west of Nurse's hotel, Duck's Wimbleton House provided an extensive "pleasure" ground with species of bears, ducks and racoons. Travellers could arrive by train or on steamers like the Canadian which departed the wharf at the foot of Spadina Avenue, or tie up their boats at Duck's private wharf. His open-air ox roasts, complete with music were wildly popular and often ended in drunken brawls.

As streetcar service developed along Lakeshore Road, and as new communities such as the railway town of New Toronto brought more development to the lakeshore, Humber Bay became engulfed, and was soon another Toronto suburb. In the 1920s, with the start of the Sunnyside Palace Pier project, a $1.25 million scheme, the area would have seen the building of a 550-metre pier, auditorium and dance hall. Delayed and

25

downscaled by the depression, the Palace Pier finally opened in 1941 and hosted international dance bands led by Les Brown, the Dorsey Brothers and Duke Ellington. In 1963 the dance hall was destroyed by fire, replaced now by the Palace Pier condominiums. The site of the old wharves meanwhile has been covered by a new park, while a modernistic pedestrian bridge now spans the historic waterway.

Long Branch

Even as Toronto was booming outward along its new streetcar lines, only a few miles from the end of the urban fringe, lay cottage country. In those pre-automobile days, when streetcars and railways were the only means of transportation, there was little development beyond that fringe. And it was here that Torontonians made their summer playground.

Prior to 1883, the Long Branch area was still farmland. But in that year James Eastwood, realizing that the pollution of the city was driving Toronto's more affluent residents to search for

Before the streetcar era, tourists travelled between Toronto and Long Branch by steamer.

26

The Hotel Long Branch featured speaking tubes: an early intercom system using tubes to relay orders or questions between rooms.

more distant summer haunts, sold his land to Thomas Wilkie who subdivided it into a 219-lot cottage community which he called Sea Breeze Park. He left the 10 acres along the lake as an open space for the purchasers to stroll. The plan consisted of a half dozen streets south of Lakeshore Road, with the main route into the area called Sea Breeze Avenue. In 1886, the first cottage was bought by Richard and May Ough. The next year the Ough's could witness the building of the magnificent Hotel Long Branch, with its Japanese balconies, and pagoda tower. Boasting electricity, speaking tubes in every room and telephone connection to Toronto, the Long Branch rented rooms for $15 per week. On the lawn by the lake stood the pavilion and the Coney Island carousel.

While many vacationers arrived by train at the Long Branch station on the Grand Trunk, most boarded steamers like the Greyhound or the White Star at the Yonge Street wharf in Toronto to sail along the lake. By 1923 streetcars were clanging along Lakeshore Road to Long Branch and many cottages

27

became permanent homes. Others were demolished in favour of more modern homes, made of sturdier brick and better insulated. Nevertheless a few of the original cottages still stand. Old summer homes can be seen at 282 and 256 Lake Promenade overlooking the park, while those at number 4 and 14 Long Branch Avenue, the current name for Sea Breeze Avenue, date from 1897 and 1890 respectively. Even the Ough cottage, now minus its decorative wrap-around porch, still overlooks the lake from Lake Promenade. Unfortunately the grandest building of the community, the elegant old hotel, burned in 1954 to be replaced by an apartment building.

Lorne Park

Like Long Branch, Lorne Park began as a summer retreat for wealthy Torontonians. But unlike Long Branch, it didn't start off as a cottage community. Instead, its first incarnation was that of an exclusive resort, or, as it was called in those times, a "pleasure ground". Here, two miles west of Oakville, on 75 acres of forested lakeshore, the Toronto Park Association opened their exclusive retreat which included a "restaurant bar parlour" with a separate parlour for ladies, bowling lanes,

Lorne Park's early activities centred around the ill-fated Lorne Park Hotel.

billiard tables and a shooting gallery, along with picnic grounds, baseball diamonds and merry-go-rounds. As with Long Branch, many vacationers arrived on the Toronto steamers.

Somewhat surprisingly, in less than a decade the enterprise was bankrupt. It was sold in 1886 to John Stackwell, who promptly subdivided the forested grounds into 50-foot building lots at $100 each. The hotel still stood, however, renamed the Hotel Louise, and leased to Thomas Anderson who operated in it the Bodega Restaurant. By 1891, 27 cottages had been built, many facing a small, square park in the centre, and claiming names like the "Buenavista" or the "Linstock Villa."

Lorne Park, however, was plagued with misfortune. The hotel still wasn't making a go of it and in 1910 became a private club for the residents, finally burning to the ground in 1920. The wharves collapsed suddenly in 1903, tossing waiting passengers into the chilly lake. By then most travellers were arriving by train at the attractive little Grand Trunk station which stood less then a mile away on Lorne Park Road. Then in 1919, beset by financial woes, the owners of the development, Lorne Park Estates, sold the stock to the cottagers themselves, and in 1923 another plan for subdivision was registered to open more lots.

Following the Second World War, the empty lots quickly filled. The opening of the QEW had brought the once remote lakeshore into Toronto's urban fold, and Lorne Park became a permanent residential nieghbourhood. The houses that now line the narrow roads display a mix of moderate, and luxury homes, while closer to the lake a few of the elegant old summer homes still stand. Two examples can be found at 892 Roper and 913 Sangster. Others face onto the little park by the lake, as they did when they were first built.

Despite the suburbanization of the area, Lorne Park still resembles a cottage community from the past. The roads, still private, are narrow, permitting only a single lane of traffic, while large shady trees cling to the roadsides, giving the appearance of driving through a forest track.

On the banks of the Rouge River the Rosebank House was a popular summer retreat for folks from West Hill and Pickering.

Rosebank

In the 1860s, when the Rouge was as distant from Toronto as Muskoka is today (and considerably less developed), Rosebank was established as a resort by John Pollock, which he later sold to William Cavan. By 1880 the families of Dr Byron Field and Alex Brown had begun to join in. In 1885 Brown built a cookhouse and sleeping house, two more being built by the Jewitts and Woodleys around 1889.

The Rosebank House became a popular resort hotel, enlarged in 1897 and again in 1907, adding a general store, pavilion and electricity. By then the community could number 17 cottages. Further east near the mouth of Petticoat Creek stood the summer house of William Moore, MP, an estate known as Moorelands. Built around 1913, it burned during the 1930s, the grounds later becoming part of the Petticoat Creek conservation area.

During this period, so popular had the area become that the Grand Trunk built a special station and added picnic specials to their regular trains. The Rosebank House sent a stage to meet the train and shuttle the happy holidayers the short distance to the resort.

By the time of the Second World War, many of the cottages were being converted to year-round homes, a trend that increased with the arrival of the 401 in 1958. Today, Rosebank Road has become a modern suburban street, while along Dyson and Bella Vista, mixed in with the large new houses are a few of the little wooden one time cottages, whose dwellers once enjoyed the peace and quiet of the woods and the water. The station stood at the point where Rodd Avenue still crosses the tracks. Further along Rodd, on the site of the Rosebank House, there stands a senior's residence, while at what was Moorelands, the steps and some foundation from the Moore mansion can be seen in the Petticoat Creek conservation area.

Summer does, however, still bring crowds to the banks of the Rouge. On the west bank a conservation area has been created along the beach on Lake Ontario, and the marsh preserved. Bathers, fishermen, and wildlife watchers carry on the summer tradition started by the Rosebank cottagers, even though the area is now entirely within Toronto's suburban cloak. It even has a new station, the Rouge Hill GO station.

> Frenchman's Bay's most popular product was ice, cut every winter by the Lake Simcoe Ice and Fuel Company, and delivered by horsedrawn wagons.

Fairport

The story of this bay community is tied up with that of the village of Dunbarton on Kingston Road, and described in the Kingston Road chapter. In fact its story takes over where that of Dunbarton leaves off. After J.T. Dunbar, who founded the village that took his name, realized that the wharves he had constructed at the north end of Frenchman's Bay were too silted, he constructed new facilities closer to the lake. Here, on the east side of the bay, a townsite was laid out and named Fairport. It contained a store, post office, two hotels, and several workers' houses, most of the development being centred around the intersection of Front and Commercial Street. By the water were the wharves, the grain elevators and the ice houses of the Simcoe Ice and Fuel Company. A number of independent fishermen also operated out of Fairport.

31

When the Grand Trunk Railway built its line through the area in 1856, shipping from Fairport dropped drastically. Sucumbing to heavy lobbying, the government pumped more than $80,000 into replacing the wharf, adding a barley elevator, and dredging the channel through the sand spit. However, the U.S. tariff against barley spelt ruin for the port, and the facilities were finally closed. The grain elevator stood until 1915 when it was torn down, although commercial fishing was still being carried out in the 1920s.

During the prohibition of the 1920s, "commerce" returned to the waters of Frenchman's Bay, and a rum runner named "Black Jack" began using the dormant port to smuggle liquor into Ontario. The police, however, caught wind of the operation, and in true "Untouchables" fashion, gunned him down following a late-night ambush. In the years leading up to the First World War, urbanites discovered "Frenchman's Bay" and began to build small cottages on the sand spit and through the townsite.

During the 1950s, with the arrival of the 401, many cottages were converted into permanent homes. Through the 1960s and 70s urban development engulfed the land around the old cottage community, and Fairport became another Toronto suburb.

This is only one of a few buildings to survive from the era when the suburb of Frenchman's Bay was a little port called Fairport.

But a few vestiges of its early era can yet be found. At the northwest corner of Wharf and Liverpool Road stands one of the old hotels, while at the south east corner, a one-time store. On the north end of the bay, the pilings of the original wharves, looking like mere stumps, still protrude from the water. On the north side of Bayly Street, at about the same point, a stone culvert cuts under the Canadian National railway tracks. This represents the original road that led from the original docks to the village of Dunbarton. However, the street was closed decades ago when CN added more tracks. One of Fairport's oldest houses, that built by the O'Briens in the 1850s, now stands at the corner of Bayview and Front, having been moved from its original site on the sand spit. On the grounds of the East Shore marina, a dance hall pavilion built during the 1930s still stands. The little store that once served as a summer post office during the 1920s survives yet on Front Street near Bayview.

The origin of the name Frenchman's Bay? Likely after Sulpician priest, François de Fénélon, who wintered there in 1669 with a band of Seneca, nearly starving to death, and Marquis Denonville who stayed there in 1687.

Todmorden Mills

2.

∽

Early Pioneer Paths

Most of the roads in the Toronto area have one distin-guishing feature. They are dead straight, following early survey lines that had no regard for rivers, lakes or hills. In fact, the survey lines were intended less for roads, and more to lay out a neat grid of farm parcels. What were called "concession roads" went along the front of the farm lots, the "side roads" connecting the concession roads every five lots or so. Many of the Toronto area's major roads still follow these farm roads: Queen Street, originally Lot Street, was the first concession road to be laid out; Bloor, St Clair, Eglinton, Lawrence and York Mills, all represent concession roads north of Queen. Airport Road traces an old farm lane once known as the Sixth Line. Rexdale Boulevard follows the Richview Side Road. Even the QEW follows an early concession road known as the Middle Road. As straight as they were, concession roads didn't always connect as neatly as they should, resulting in sud-den kinks and doglegs. Each township had a different system of surveying, sometimes a result of starting at a different base line, sometimes a result of a different pattern of farm land sur-veys. Scarborough for example had rectangular farm blocks, while those is Toronto were square, and in North York, trape-zoidal. Not surprisingly, when the farm roads met at the town-ship boundaries, the connections were not exact. Most have been smoothed out with the massive road realignments that accompanied the car craze and the suburban boom of the post war years.

A few roads, however, stand out from this pattern by winding their way over the countryside as a drunk might wind his way through a crowd. For example, some of the first interurban roads, like Lakeshore Road or the Danforth Road, followed Indian trails, or simply the lay of the land. Others were the shortcuts that the pioneers followed to get to the mills or to the markets where the surveyed farm roads proved inconvenient. These included streets known today as Broadview, Davenport, Dawes, Albion, and a few that have nearly vanished completely.

DON MILLS ROAD

Don Vale

One of Toronto's early east end roads was Don Mills Road. Most modern-day Metro-ites picture a six-lane suburban road that slices through the back splits and high-rises of North York, finally ending just beyond the Don Valley Parkway near O'Connor. At first, none of that route was "Don Mills Road". Rather, a road known as the "Mill Road", according to the earliest maps, began at today's Winchester Street, and Parliament Street, tracing Winchester eastward to the necropolis where it descended

Peter Lamb's repugnant glue and blacking factory discouraged residential development near its Amelia Street location. The spire of the necropolis chapel is in the background.

into the Don Valley. It then remounted the eastern wall of the valley, skirting it to Pottery Road where it descended to the site of the "Don Mills", known later as Todmorden Mills. A few years later, the name "Don Mills Road" was given to Broadview Avenue from Queen Street northward, and to O'Connor as far as today's Don Mills Road, where the extensive Taylor Mills complex stood at the fork of the Don River's two branches.

Travelling on Toronto's early pioneer roads was as much a pub crawl as it was a voyage, and taverns appeared at frequent intervals. From the site of the Santa Claus Hotel, occupied today by the Winchester Hotel (still standing) journeyers need only to reach the bottom of the valley where they could pause once more for refreshment in the Don Vale House. By the time they made it back up the east side, and through Doncaster, just north of today's intersection of Danforth Avenue and Broadview, they could sip once more in one of the two taverns that marked Todmorden.

Don Vale, up until the 1870s and 80s, was more a scattered rural community than it was a clustered village. It consisted of the Santa Claus Hotel at Winchester and Parliament, some country homes along the Mill Road (Winchester), the necropolis, and at the foot of the hill below the necropolis, the Fox Head Hotel, which later became known as the Don Vale House, giving the community its name.

An early and most unpleasant industry here was the Peter Lamb glue and blacking factory located at the east end of Amelia Street. Operating from the late 1840s to the 1890s, it cremated animals to manufacture glue. Although Lamb built a few cabins for his workers, the presence of this noxious operation discouraged residential development in the area.

Although some speculation had taken place as early as the 1850s, development was not feasible until the 1880s, when a rush of immigration from the British Isles brought workers looking for housing near the factories by the tracks at the foot of Parliament Street. By the turn of the century, Don Vale had become the newest suburb in a rapidly growing and rapidly industrializing Toronto, and the rural community disappeared.

A few vestiges of rural Don Vale are still evident today. By the 1890s John Ayre's Lakeview Hotel had replaced the Santa Claus, and had achieved a reputation as "an excellent up-town hotel . . . rapidly growing in favour as a resort for the travelling public and families." It was praised for its good lawn, telephone and convenient access to all parts of the city. Although it was nearly a mile from the lake, a view of the water was possible from its belvedere. Renamed the Winchester Hotel, it still dominates the intersection, and is now a local pub.

The oldest building in Don Vale is the Charles Parson House at 85 Winchester, just a short distance east of the hotel. It was built in the 1850s as a country home for a local leather merchant. At the time he could enjoy an unimpeded view north to St. James Cemetery, and east to the necropolis. Another two blocks further east stands the beautiful Daniel Lamb House, set back from the sidewalk. When it was built for the son of the owner of the Lamb factory in 1867, it was still only one of ten houses on Winchester Street. A little further east, and a few paces south on Sumach, stands a contemporary of the Lamb house, Number 384, built in 1866 and known as the "Witch's House." South and east of Sumach and Winchester is another long-established Toronto institution, the Riverdale Zoo. It was conceived by Daniel Lamb in 1899, then an alderman for the City of Toronto. From a lonely polar bear and a couple of wolves, the zoo grew into a popular destination for children from all across the city. When the Metro Zoo opened in Scarborough in 1978, Riverdale became a petting farm, with livestock, barn and historic farmhouse moved in from Markham.

Across the street is the Toronto Necropolis. It dates from 1852 when development pressures in Yorkville forced the potter's field burying ground to move from there to this site. The Victorian Gothic chapel was designed by Henry Langley in 1872. Beyond the chapel, Winchester ends and "Mill Road" becomes a service lane for the Riverdale Farm. At the base of the hill upon which the necropolis sits, the road ends at the Bayview Extension, marking the approximate site of the Don

When it was built in 1867, Daniel Lamb's house, on what is now Winchester Street, was a country home.

Vale house. It had remained a popular "sporting" tavern, with fighting and gambling, until it closed in 1880. It was torn down two decades later.

The site of the repulsive Lamb "glue factory", at the east end of Amelia Street, is now a pleasant park, and a common front yard for a row of early 1900s town houses. The Lamb factory manufactured glue, ground bone, animal charcoal, and a shoe and stove lustre known as Lamb's Penny Blacking. The main building burned in 1888, and by 1900 the site had become a park. A few workers' cabins yet stand on Amelia Street east of Sumach.

The Don Vale area, erroneously called "Cabbagetown", (an Irish neighbourhood which was actually south of Gerrard), is one of Toronto's most strollable residential neighbourhoods. Its streets are crammed with an astounding mix of 1880s and 90s tiny workers' cabins, and grand upper-middle-class homes, often side by side. The "gentrification" of the area that began in the 1960s has meant the retention of the historic homes and streetscapes, and the development of a strong sense of pride in the area's heritage.

Chester

In those days the east end's best known street, Danforth
Avenue was scarcely known at all. While most traffic slugged its
way along Kingston Road or Don Mills Road, the Danforth
remained a muddy and lightly used farm lane, laid out as the
first concession road north of Kingston Road. Only when the
magnificent Bloor Viaduct was opened in 1920 did develop-
ment start to engulf the area, and in less than two decades
Danforth became the longest commercial strip in the entire
Toronto area. Until then, the only link to the city was, first, via
Mill Road, which wound down the valley and up and through
Don Vale. Then, in 1889, streetcars began clanging along
Queen Street and up Broadview which took over the name
"Don Mills Road".

Before streetcars provided this vital link, a trio of rural farm
villages grew up in the area to serve the local population:
Todmorden on the Don Mills Road above the Taylor Mills,
Coleman Corners to the east, and at Don Mills and Danforth,
the hamlet of Chester.

Not surprisingly, the village of Chester developed initially
around a couple of taverns, the Priestly tavern at the intersection, and Danforth Hall, a short distance east. A mile east of
that the "Dutch Farm" was earning a wide reputation for its
meals of sausage and brown bread. Also known as Doncaster
Post Office, the community was a busy village laid out along
Don Mills just north of Danforth. The name "Chester" was
bestowed upon it by the rector of the Norway Church, James
Beaven, when he opened a mission there (after Chester,
England). Along the street were James Young's general store,
James Arnold's blacksmith shop and St. Barnabas church, a
board-and-batten structure built around 1860. It was replaced
in 1918 by a new brick building on Hampton Ave, a building
which still stands.

By the 1890s, Chester could also count eight small brick-
yards. Among the earliest were those of Whitmore and
Stotebury on the east side of Broadview between Sparkhall and
Hogarth, lasting from the 1840s until 1870. However, by the

1930s, all the brickyards had ceased operation, except one — the Toronto Brick Yards, whose buildings yet stand on the north side of the Bayview Extension, south of Pottery Road.

With the streetcars came the land speculators. In 1890, the residents of Chester along with those in Todmorden petitioned for incorporation as a village in order to service the land for development. But because even together, the communities were short of the 750 resident population needed, their request was denied.

Finally in 1912, with the prospect of a new bridge over the Don Valley and annexation to Toronto, the area's largest landowners, the Playters, began to subdivide their large holdings. As far back as 1793, Captain George Playter, army officer and Loyalist, had been granted 500 acres of land near the Don River. A 200-acre parcel, deeded to his son, James, lay at the northeast corner of today's Danforth and Broadview. Earlier they had severed off individual parcels to help create the village of Chester. The Playter Estates, as the subdivision was called, became an attractive community of curving streets and handsome homes. The neighbourhood still retains both the appearance and the name. In its midst stands the Playter farmhouse, built around 1870.

Streetcars

Before widespread electrical power, public transit took the form of horsedrawn buggies, fit into steel tracks raised from the street. Despite having to switch to sleighs in winter, the system was effective and popular. Electric streetcars were introduced in Toronto in 1885, but the first full-fledged electric tram system in Ontario began operating in Windsor, in 1886.

But the Playter Estates marked the beginning of the end for Chester. With the opening of the long-awaited Bloor Viaduct in 1920, development swept through the area like a wind-driven wildfire, and within a few years, the Danforth had become Toronto's longest commercial street. The farms utterly vanished, and side streets leading north and south became working-class neighbourhoods. Now, apartments, stores, and a new streetcar terminal have replaced the community's early buildings. Only the name survives on the walls of the Chester subway station.

Todmorden

Less than a mile north of Chester on Don Mills Road, the traveller came to the village of Todmorden. While the Todmorden Mills stood down in the valley, a separate village grew along the busy roadway above, between what are today's Pottery Road and O'Connor. The early directories listed two general stores, two blacksmiths, and the taverns. The Todmorden Hotel stood at Broadview and Pottery, replacing an earlier hotel at the northeast corner of Broadview and Eastwood. Here farmers would line up, sometimes 60 or 70 teams, to use the weigh scale in front of the hotel, and then retire inside for lunch and a beverage. Behind the Todmorden stood Hugh Ried's blacksmith shop, while behind the former tavern was Donald's blacksmith shop. After 1855, when the Taylor family aquired the Todmorden Mills, they built some of the village's grandest homes. Among the most luxurious was the mansion called Chester Park estate.

Although forced to turn dry during prohibition, the Todmorden Hotel became a popular gambling den. During this period it was owned by Robert Davies who also owned 144 other taverns, the Don Brewery, Coplands Brewery, the Don Valley Brick Works, and the Taylor Paper Factory, an empire worth $9 million.

An early focus for village activity, the historic Todmorden Hotel stood near the intersection of today's Broadview and Pottery Road.

Built in 1885, John Taylor's mansion still dominates the vista along a modern-looking Broadview Avenue.

Because Chester remained the end of streetcar service, the residential tide did not sweep through Todmorden until the 1930s. Amid the sturdy, little brick bungalows, and the later apartments, several of Todmorden's old buildings still stand. Number 1132 Broadview marks the site of the Taylor's Chester Park Mansion, later aquired by Davies after he had married into the Taylor family. The manison was demolished in the 1940s, and only the coach house remains today. Despite the loss of Chester Park, the mansion of John F. Taylor dominates the view along Broadview. Now a senior citizen's home, this 1885 Queen-Anne-style mansion is located at 2 O'Connor. Nearby, the buildings at 1232-4 Broadview contained a general store operated by David Cramp, while beside it, 1224-28 once housed a hotel.

Todmorden consisted of another village cluster as well. A half mile east of Broadview, Beechwood Avenue once led to the Taylor's Middle Mills. At 20-22 Beechwood, north of O'Connor, stands one of Todmorden's most important buildings, second only to the mill complex itself. Built in 1840 in the simple

Beechwood was one of the earlier Taylor family mansions. It still stands.

Regency style of the period, it is the mansion originally owned by George Taylor, one of the founders of the Taylor Paper Company. Nearby stands a trio of Taylor workers' houses. They are situated east of the Taylor Mansion, at Number 9, 11, and 13 Hassard Street, and date from the 1850s-70s. Although unrelated to the mill operation itself, a few paces south, at 89 Woodville, stands another of Todmorden's early houses, a fine brick residence built in 1888 by Mrs Alice Woolfrey, a large property owner at that time.

Two blocks east of the Taylor mansion stood the Todmorden church. Here, at the northwest corner of today's Pape and O'Connor (what would have been Don Mills and Leslie, then), the Don Mills United Church occupies the ground donated by George Taylor in 1859, and contains the graves of the Taylor, the Helliwell and the Skinner families.

Helping to preserve a sense of history in this historic community, the East York Local Advisory Committee on Architectural Conservation (LACAC) has published a Historic Walking Tour of Todmorden which includes the mill complex and other buildings of interest in the general area.

DAWES ROAD

Coleman's Corners

Dawes Road was one of those roads that began as a short cut. A cow path, it gave farmers a shorter connection between Kingston Road and the farmlands then opening in northern Scarborough. Originally, Dawes Road ran from Kingston Road near today's Main St. It angled northeastwardly until it reached what is now Victoria Park Avenue, a little below its intersection with St. Clair, continuing north along today's Victoria Park alignment to Wexford, located at Lawrence Avenue. At the time, "Victoria Park Avenue", named for a popular park on the lake, did not extend north of Danforth Avenue.

Dawes, at first, was not a legal road, for it failed to follow the surveyed farm roads. Finally, in 1848, Dawes Road was legally opened to traffic. Where it crossed Danforth Avenue, a cross-roads hamlet developed, consisting of the typical cluster of hotels. On the northwest corner stood the hotel operated by Clem Dawes, and after whom the Dawes Road was named. George Coleman ran the Eastbourne Hotel on the southeast corner, and gave his name to the hamlet itself. However, the

George Empringham's hotel was one of several clustered around Danforth Avenue and Dawes Road called Coleman's Corners.

45

largest establishment was that of George Empringham. This three storey brick building stood on the southwest corner, and had a wrap-around porch. Although moved back from its original location, it stood until the 1980s, later known as the Danforth Hotel, complete with exotic dancers, when it was destroyed by fire and replaced with a small group of uninteresting shops. On the north west corner of Danforth and Dawes was the Little York Hotel, also known as the White House or Evan Hotel.

One of the better-known hotels, however, stood a little west of the corners. At the northwest corner of Danforth and Westlake, Charles Gates (brother of Jonathan, who operated a hotel on Kingston Road) ran not just a hotel, but a racetrack. The Newmarket Race Course was a mile-long track which sprawled behind the hotel. Named after the famous Newmarket racetracks in England, Gates' course hosted the Queens Plate in 1868. However, when the Woodbine Race Track on Kingston Road opened in 1874, Gates's course became a mere training track, and with the land boom on the Danforth a few years later,

Traffic on the Danforth, here at Coleman's Corners, was congested even in "horse and buggy" days.

46

was removed to make way for housing. Gates Avenue and Newmarket Avenue are named in memory of Charles Gates and his race track. During this period these hotels were considered to be "suburban hotels", and as Toronto's urban fringe crept closer, they became popular with up-scale urbanites, out for a weekend of dining, dancing or cycling.

Following the opening of the Bloor Viaduct, development spread east and soon absorbed Coleman's Corners. While the Empringham Hotel is gone, two others yet survive amid the chaos of the Danforth's commercial clutter. They are the "White House" hotel, visible behind a cut-rate furniture store west of Dawes Road, and, on the southeast corner, Coleman's old hotel, now a popular pub by the name of Noah's.

Little York

By 1856, the Grand Trunk had laid its line parallel to the Danforth, crossing Dawes Road south of Coleman's Corners. But in 1883, then in the process of gobbling up smaller lines, the railway was looking for more space to put its sorting yards. A large, flat area south of Coleman's Corners proved ideal. Here it cut off Dawes Road, and south of the yards, superimposed a planned railway town it called East Toronto.

While most of the railway workers lived in typical railway housing in the new town, a new community also grew up north of Coleman's Corners. Taking the name of the Grand Trunk's York Station, it was called "Little York". Mainly a residential community, Little York's only industry was the brick making operation run by the Newman family. Most of the residential subdivision lay east of Dawes and north of the Danforth.

A latecomer to Little York was another railway line. The Canadian Northern Railway, deciding, fatefully in 1911, to build Ontario's third main line east of Toronto, laid their rails up the Taylor Creek ravine, crossing Dawes road on a bridge where the hydro wires cross today. But three such railways were excessive, for the CPR and the Grand Trunk also had lines running east, and the Canadian Northern was gone after just 20 years. Although the railway's timetables do not record a station for this location, area residents hold that a building on Midburn Avenue was once a ticket office for the railway. Although the railway bridge across Dawes Road has long been removed, the right-of-way remains clearly evident.

During its years as a rail workers' community, Little York "enjoyed" a rough and tumble reputation. Its residents took great pride in their soccer team which bested such touted teams as the Toronto Thistles on the field located north of the tracks and east of Dawes Road.

Coleman's Corners was absorbed by East Toronto, and then by Toronto itself. Little York, meanwhile, remained within East York. It lost its separate identity during the 1920s as the housing boom spread east along the Danforth and later in the 1960s as apartment development spread down Dawes Road from north of Taylor Creek.

A number of houses built before Little York vanished still stand on these streets. The two most important are the large Gothic Revival house at 122 Dawes Road, built in 1885 and owned by the Newman family from 1910 until 1976. The Newmans, who operated a brickyard on the north side of the Taylor Creek ravine, also owned a number of lots along Midburn Avenue, the community's main street east of Dawes Road, where the attractive 1900 home of Margaret McKinnon still stands at Number 5.

The Goulding estate still stands on Dawes Road.

A prominent feature on the landscape of Little York was the Goulding estate of the prestigious Massey family, whose large dairy farm straddled the banks of Taylor Creek east of Dawes Road. Here, in 1927, Walter Massey's daughter, Mrs Dorothy Goulding, built the palatial estate house at 305 Dawes Road designed by architect F.H. Marani. In 1965 the Goulding estate sold their land to developers, and a decade later sold the house to the Metro Toronto Children's Aid Society. Although it has lost some of its grandeur, the beautiful

Tudor-style building still stands in the midst of wooded grounds, singularly out of place in the sea of apartments.

Moffat's Corners

Known as Strangford Post Office, Moffat's Corners existed at the corner of St. Clair and Dawes Road (now Victoria Park Avenue). Travellers journeying north along Dawes Road would pause here at the Royal Oak Inn opened by Alexander and Thomas Moffatt in 1845 before continuing on into northern Scarborough. St. Clair Avenue then continued only a short distance west before ending at the Boyd Farm, located where the community of Parkview Hills now sits. As a result there was little incentive for the hamlet to grow, and Strangford contained little other than the tavern, a Methodist church at St. Clair and Pharmacy, and a few cabins.

Then in 1888 the closing of Dawes Road at the Grand Trunk tracks blocked any traffic that would have come from Kingston Road. The little crossroads hamlet lost its importance and vanished, the tavern lasting until 1947 when it burned. With the suburban boom that followed the Second World War, St. Clair was opened to O'Connor and widened to four lanes, while housing has filled-in the farm fields. The intersection is much busier now, with a pharmacy, a discount food store, a McDonalds and a tavern on the four corners. Other than a single former cabin south of the intersection, there is no evidence that a hamlet ever existed here at all.

DAVENPORT ROAD

Davenport

Originally an Indian trail, Davenport Road predated Simcoe's planned roads of Dundas Street, Kingston Road, and Yonge Street. Yet development along it did not take place until the 1840s when immigration began to sweep through Southern Ontario's farmlands. By all accounts, however, the land along this section was less fertile, and attracted fewer farmers. Its route led northwestward from Yorkville on Yonge Street, following the base of a bluff to a junction with Weston Road. Despite the poor quality soils, the views from the high bluff attracted Toronto's wealthy class to construct what were then some of the city's most spectacular country homes. From the heights of the cliffs, the 19th-century gentry could gaze from their balustrades over the forested flats to the sparkling lake waters a mile away. Two such palaces that are open to the public include the Spadina House museum, and its more famous neighbour, Casa Loma.

Two hamlets also appeared along Davenport Road, one near today's Symington Avenue, the hamlet of Davenport, the other near St. Clair Avenue and Weston Road, the community of Carlton.

Davenport began with the construction of the Ontario Simcoe and Huron Railway in 1853. In that year George Cooper donated a portion of his land for the building of a railway station, a device used by many landowners during the railway building era. While the railways were only too happy to accept free land, the presence of a station dramatically increased the value of the donor's property and allowed him to subdivide the rest of his land.

The village developed along the road and included Rowntree's store, a blacksmith shop and a hotel operated by Thomas Tuey. In 1871, James English was the ticket agent for the Grand Trunk Railway, which had by then assumed the line, while Joseph Green was the station master.

Davenport station was an attractive English-style country station with a steeply pitched roof and decorative gable. The building was considered a Toronto landmark and frequently featured in 19th century publications on the Toronto area. It was eventually replaced around the turn of the century by the station on the north side of St Clair Avenue, which sat neglected in recent years until it was destroyed by fire in 1997.

Toronto's urban growth struck the area around the turn of the century, and came from a couple of different angles. While some development was spreading northwestward on Davenport itself, a bustling new railway town had appeared across the CPR

This attractive English-style railway station spurred the development of the hamlet of Davenport.

tracks: West Toronto Junction. In fact, both Carlton and Davenport became part of the town of West Toronto before being absorbed into Toronto itself.

Three other buildings date from the days when Davenport was a country village. At the southwest corner of Davenport and Symington, the brick buildings occupied by the Good Boy chinese restaurant and Mr K Convenience represent the 1887 Rowntree store which once contained the Davenport post office. Further west, the United Church, which was built in 1901, marks the site of Cooper's original 1857 church site. Across the street, on the southwest corner of Perth, behind the Oshanti's Herbal Store, stands the church manse built for the local Anglican pastor, the Reverend C.E. Thompson, in 1889. Meanwhile, the Northern Railway was double tracked, the level crossing replaced by a bridge, and the station ground taken over by warehouses.

The streets in the old village area bear distinctive "Davenport Village" signs that identify them as once having been part of a village now engulfed by urban growth.

Carlton

Before the railways arrived, and before the village of Davenport appeared, Carlton existed as a community just north of the junction of Dundas Street and Weston Road (then known as Royce Road). One of the area's earliest hotels was the two-storey-wooden Peacock Tavern at the junction itself.

In 1867, at the intersection of what is today St. Clair and Weston Road, Henry Royce operated the toll gate that charged farmers to travel between the mills at Weston, and the market in York. As often occurred around toll gates, a small crossroads community grew up, starting with the ever-present tavern, a story-and-a-half rough-cast building known as the Durham Heifer Hotel. In 1856, the Grand Trunk laid the rails for its Point Edward line a short distance to the west of the cross-roads, and named the station Carlton West. Here, in 1867, Frances Heydon moved from Kleinburg and bought the dilap-idated Durham Heifer, renaming it the Carlton. Across from it stood a carriage factory operated by John Alfred Bull, Peter Mallaby's blacksmith, and another tavern known as Brown's

Toll gates such as this on Davenport Road were hated by those forced to use them. Davenport Road follows an early native trail linking the Humber and Don Rivers.

Inn, run by a family of ex-slaves from Maryland. North of the Carlton Hotel, George Townsley began a brick-making operation which by the 1890s was turning out a million bricks a year.

With the arrival of the Toronto Grey and Bruce Railway in the 1880s, the area became a busy junction, and in 1890 Francis Heydon's son, Alex, hired architect James Ellis to replace the tired, old hotel with a grand, new brick building. Ellis' design was widely hailed. The West Toronto Tribune described the Heydon House in 1898 as "palatial, having a handsome and imposing exterior and its interior arrangement is admirably adapted to the comfort and convenience of the guests." It contained 25 rooms, a ballroom and dining room. It quickly became popular with cycling and sleighing excursionists, while the second floor "ballroom" witnessed a number of illegal cockfights.

Francis Heydon and John Bull had become the area's political leaders, and in the 1880s began to lobby for village status for both Carlton and Davenport, under the name "Stanley." However, a land dispute between Stanley and the neighbouring village of West Toronto led to the county council rejecting the bid until the dispute was resolved. Rather than continue to fight, however, Stanley simply amalgamated with Toronto Junction to become "West Toronto Junction". Two decades later, the "City of West Toronto" was annexed by the City of Toronto.

While West Toronto, or "The Junction" remains a distinct and proud community, the hamlets of Davenport and Carlton have vanished into the mists of time. As have most of their buildings. New commercial development now dominates three of Carlton's four old crossroads corners. The Grand Trunk's Carlton station was removed to make way for track expansion and replaced in 1890 with a newer West Toronto station adjacent to Weston Road. Although gutted by fire in 1994, it still stands in ruin, its future bleak. Meanwhile, the historic Heydon House has enjoyed a happier fate and in 1983 it was designated an historic building by the City of Toronto. Although it still dominates the northwest corner of St. Clair and Weston Road, as it has for over a century, it is now missing part of its elegant tower.

ALBION ROAD

Thistletown

Although settlement moved rapidly along the shore of Lake Ontario, the pace of pioneering was stalled to the northwest. Roads like Islington Avenue, originally called Middle Road, and Albion Road, then the Claireville Road, had been surveyed as early as 1799, and lots were laid out to await their owners, but remained impassible quagmires. Then, with the immigration waves in the 1820s and 1840s, the frontier began to move again.

As the area rang to the sound of axes felling the primeval forests, a hotel, general store and blacksmith appeared at the intersection of Albion and Islington. The cluster was named Conat's Corners, after one of the first families. In 1847, Scottish immigrant John Grubb laid out a small village he called St. Andrews. Because of confusion with St. Andrews in New Brunswick, the post office gave it the name Thistletown, after Dr. William Thistle, the local doctor whose son, John Thistle, just happened to be the postmaster. To improve the road and encourage settlement in his new village, Grubb started the Albion Plank Road Company

Thistletown retained many of its early hamlet buildings even into the 1950s. None of these structures at Islington Avenue and Albion Road have survived.

As Grubb's lots filled in, Thistletown grew to include Thistle's general store on the northeast corner, a butcher shop on the southeast corner, and the Albion Hotel on the southwest corner. With its large adjoining ballroom, and stables capable of housing a hundred horses, the Albion was a popular feature with farmers carrying their grain to the mills on the Humber at Weston.

An interesting feature of Thistletown was the Village Green Park. An open area donated by Jonathan Farr in 1896, it, along with the school and community hall, provided an opportunity for the villagers to hold various social events. The school was built in 1874, and the hall added in 1910.

Although Thistletown failed to attract either the Northern Railway or the Toronto Grey and Bruce Railway, both of which passed through Weston, Thistletown's location on a busy road allowed it to continue to bustle. But it's face was changed forever following the end of the Second World War. The Auto Era ushered in a suburban land boom, and old Thistletown stood right in the way. Both Albion and Islington were widened and, in the case of Albion Road, straightened, sweeping away many of the area's historic buildings. Small plazas and donut shops replaced the general store and hotel while subdivisions covered the farm fields. Fortunately, the village side streets were spared, and on them, near the corner of Riverdale and Jason Streets, stands the community's most historic structure. Number 23 Jason, a stone house built before 1820, and possibly as early as 1802, was occupied by John Grubb himself until his new home was completed in 1834. That new home was a handsome story-and-a-half stuccoed Regency cottage that Grubb called Elm Bank. It is known as Number 19 Jason, and is attached to the rear of number 23. Number 32 and 34 Jason also owed their history to Grubb, the latter originally used by Grubb to house his pig stock and later converted to a residence, the former having been built on the foundation of Grubb's barn.

Plank Roads

Common in the mid 19th century, the plank road was a Canadian invention, devised to ease travel on timber-strewn and potholed pioneer paths.

John Grubb's historic Elm Bank residence is part of this elegant stone house in Thistletown.

Meanwhile, east of Albion Road, Edgebrook and Bankfield Streets represent the original alignment of the pioneer trail where it made its way up the west wall of the Humber Valley (east branch). And on the floor of the flood plain, where buildings are no longer permitted, an orchard survives as a reminder of Thistletown's rural roots.

Smithfield

Further west along the Plank Road, the hamlet of Smithfield grew around the intersection of the Second Line, today's Martin Grove Road. Named after Robert Smith, who in 1839 donated land for a church, it grew to contain the Olive store on the southwest corner, and beside it Jeremiah Brook's black-smith shop. In 1874 a typical, little red school house was built on the north side of Albion Road to replace an earlier log structure that stood on the south side. Sadly, that historic institution was burned by vandals in 1957.

Smithfield's church was located a distance to the east on the "Little Concession," or Islington Avenue, but it too is gone, demolished for new development.

Claireville's Queens Hotel is now gone.

Claireville

Located at the intersection of two busy pioneer roads, the Indian Line, and the Albion Plank Road, one of the first businesses to locate here was a pub, opened in 1832 by John Dark. Claireville went on to add a Congregational church, a store and a blacksmith shop. By 1850 it had three churches and two hotels, and by 1877 could claim 175 residents.

The railways, however, gave Clairville a wide berth, and it declined. By the 1970s the only village functions that remained, besides private homes, were a church, a store, and the community hall. Today it doesn't have even that, and by 1997 was down to just nine buildings, all residences. Situated at the corner of Alcide and Codlin, it is virtually isolated by a triangle of busy roads that includes Steeles, Highway 427 and Highway 407. By 1997, rezoning signs were perched on the fringes of the place, indicating that it would disappear further.

57

Deer Park

3

The Villages of Yonge Street

Call it "Fun Street", call it Main Street Canada, call it the "world's longest road," Yonge Street is arguably Ontario's best known street and one of its oldest. It was a route which the governor of the day, John Graves Simcoe, considered to be its most important.

If he was to provide Canada with its best defence, Simcoe needed a quick route from Lake Ontario to the upper Great Lakes, one that avoided the American border. From Toronto's harbour he had a choice of two routes, one that followed the Humber River, known as the "Toronto Carrying Place," the other which followed the Don River. Because it was shorter, Simcoe chose the latter

Surveying began in 1794 but hit a snag when the natives claimed that the land was still theirs. Surveyor Augustus Jones resolved the impediment when he married the daughter of a well-known chief. Along with a group of Queen's Rangers, Jones cleared about four miles north from today's Eglinton Avenue. William Berczy and three dozen of his prospective settlers then pitched in and cleared more of the route, taking him one third of the way to Holland Landing, the road's immediate destination. But Berczy became more interested in constructing a canal along the Rouge to his settlers' land than in clearing Yonge Street, and the road building once more ground to halt, this time near today's Langstaff..

William Berczy

William Berczy was much more than a colonizer. He was best known, in fact, for his painting and architecture. He designed the Christ Church in Montreal in 1803, and painted many portraits, most notably that of Joseph Brant, considered a masterpiece.

59

His health failing, Simcoe ordered the Rangers to continue where Berczy had left off. He then returned home to England where he died shortly thereafter. By 1800 Yonge Street was officially open, but was ". . . as yet very bad; pools of water roots of trees and fallen logs, being half frozen render them still more disagreeable when horses plunge into them." Eventually conditions improved and it became the main artery that Simcoe had intended, attracting an average of a tavern a mile. Around these all-important watering holes, hamlets developed. Some of them grew while others stagnated, and a few quickly dropped from sight. Today, they count among Toronto's lost villages. Most, however, have left some vestiges of their days as separate little pioneer gathering spots.

Yorkville

For many years, Yorkville, a country settlement well north of York, began, as did many early villages, around a toll gate. Toll gates more often than not led to taverns, and taverns to towns. Yorkville fit this pattern. The toll gate appeared around 1796 and within a dozen years, Daniel Tiers had opened the Red Lion Inn (on the east side of Yonge, just north of today's Bloor Street). A small stream known as Severn's Creek, a short distance to the northeast, contained enough flow of water to power industry. The first to locate there was a brewery erected by Joseph Bloor in 1830, which stood beside today's Rosedale Valley Road, west of the Sherbourne Street bridge. A few years later, closer to Yonge Street, John Severn added a second brewery. But along with industry came the land speculators, and Sheriff William Jarvis, after whom Jarvis Street is named, was one. On land northwest of the corner of Yonge and the First Concession (Bloor Street), Jarvis laid out Yorkville. Development, however, remained slow. It was too far to travel to the factories in Toronto, which were heavily concentrated along the lake. But in 1849 omnibus service made commuting easier and Yorkville began to grow. In 1852, "1,000" petitioners asked for village status although far fewer than that actually lived there. A nearby cemetery, it is speculated, "contributed" heavily to the petition. Nevertheless, Yorkville officially became a village, with its shops concentrated largely on Yonge Street, although its village streets stretched as far west as today's Avenue Road, and north to Davenport. Bay Street had not been extended through the townsite at that time.

One of the first acts of the new council was to create a coat of arms, the second to commission the building of a town hall. Completed in 1860, the hall stood on Yonge opposite today's Collier Street, and was constructed of stone from the Credit Valley quarries. Its tower remained a Yonge Street landmark for many decades,with the coat of arms that included a symbol for the occupations of each member of that first council. The hall was gutted by fire in 1941, and demolished the following year. The coat of arms, however, was rescued and sits to this day on the tower of the Yorkville Fire Hall. Now the most prominent of Yorkville's landmarks, the fire tower, built in 1876, still stands on

Horsedrawn trolleys had just come to Yorkville when this photo looking north on Yonge Street from near Bloor was taken. The large building served as Yorkville's town hall. It burned in 1941.

The tower from the old Yorkville fire station survives on today's fire station and contains the town's old coat of arms.

Yorkville Avenue west of Yonge. The main fire hall, however, was replaced in 1889.

By 1881, Toronto was closing in on Yorkville which by then had boomed to about 5,000 residents, and extended north up Yonge to almost the Summerhill area. East of Yonge, however, a subdivision of the Rosedale estate was slower to develop. Finally, in 1883, Toronto annexed the area, and Yorkville was swallowed by this surge of urban growth. New services, like sidewalks and paved streets, appeared, as did electric street railway service, and Bay Street was extended north from Bloor to meet Davenport. Vacant lots quickly filled, and new subdivisions appeared.

Yorkville remained a quiet residential neighbourhood until the 1960s when the first of the coffee houses began to appear. With names like the Chat Noir and the Riverboat, they attracted a group of budding young folk-singers like Gordon Lightfoot, Catherine McKinnon, and Arlo Guthrie. Inevitably the area began to attract the curious, and soon became a haven for "pot-smoking hippies." Proposals to turn this street of sin into a canyon of apartments were met with concerted opposition. The old houses were saved, and soon the neighbourhood evolved into one of the Toronto area's more upscale shopping districts, frequented by visiting Hollywood stars, and likened by some to Beverly Hills' Rodeo Drive.

Several buildings, however, from Yorkville's earlier village days still stand among the new and renewed. Although nothing of that period remains on Yonge Street (though several stores on the west side of Yonge do date from the early urban days), the old fire tower remains a landmark on Yorkville just west of Yonge. Number 77 Yorkville is another old building built in 1867 for saloon keeper John Daniels. Number 100

Yorkville was built in 1881 but was best known as the Mount Sinai Hospital, a role it served from 1922 - 1952. During the heady hippy days of the sixties, it was a senior's home, where elderly citizens, some bewildered, others bemused, stared from their porch at an endless parade of "flower children."

Hazelton Avenue is Yorkville's historic north-south street, and several structures here also recall the place's more pastoral times. Houses at 49-51, 53-63, and 65-68, all date back to the 1870s. One of the most pleasing of the village's old buildings is that occupied by the Heliconian Club. Built as a Presbyterian Church, it was moved from the adjacent lot to its present site on the east side of Hazelton, a block from Yorkville Avenue. On Scollard Street, buildings at 99 - 101 and 105 were all built in the early 1870s. Most of the other houses, or converted versions, while old and attractive, followed rather than predated the urban boom.

In a way, Yorkville still serves a role much like that of its early days. Then it was an oasis, a country village far from the maddening crowd. Well, the crowds have arrived, but its pedestrian scale streetscape and its attempts at heritage preservation have kept Yorkville an oasis within what is often an overpowering urban environment.

Drummondville

From Yorkville, the early teams hauling wagons or stages would leave and struggle up the Yonge Street hill (today's Summerhill area) to a crossroads community once known as Drummondville. Here, three hotels clustered at the intersection of what became today's Yonge and St. Clair, (St. Clair being the second concession north of Lot Street). Sellers Hotel stood on the southwest corner, while that known as the Deer Park Hotel stood on the northeast. The hotel, and eventually the community itself, took its name from the Deer Park Estate that the Heath family established in 1837. The name was appropriate, for deer from the Heath estate would frequently wander over to the hotel, to the considerable amusement of the guests.

The intersection seemed important enough for one Baron Frederic de Hoen to try his hand at land speculation. At the

63

northwest corner of the intersection, he laid out a townsite which he called Drummondville, with streets that carried names like John, William, King and Queen. But by the 1850s only three owners had taken up lots, and the name was dropped.

However, the healthier air of the hillside and the wonderful views to the south proved irresistible to the gentry, anxious to feel aloof from the growing urban area. The Carthews acquired the six acres south of the Heath Estate and called it Lawton Park. But urban growth crawled irresolutely northward and in 1908 Deer Park was annexed to Toronto. Houses and stores engulfed the area, removing all traces of the early hamlet. The Sellers hotel stood on the southwest corner for many years before being demolished. The only vestiges of those days are the pillars that marked the entrance to the Carthew's Lawton Estate, and now Oriole Gardens Blvd.

Davisville

Modern-day Yonge Street continues north from "Deer Park", passing the Mount Pleasant Cemetery, beneath the railway bridge that marks the site of the ill-fated Belt Line Railway, and on to the one-time hamlet of Davisville.

The community got under way when John Davis arrived from England in 1845 and opened a pottery. Soon there were a blacksmith, general stores and a hotel clustered around the pastoral intersection. The first post office opened in Crown's grocery at the northwest corner of Imperial and Yonge, and then moved in 1894 to the Davis' store on the northeast corner of Yonge and Davisville.

But Davisville's best known, and only real industry for that matter, were the potteries. Located originally at the corner of Yonge and Millwood, the Davis' drew their clay first from an area behind the building, and then later from a clay deposit on Eglinton near the Don Valley. In 1916, needing a larger area, the Davis' moved it to where the apartments at 375 Merton are today, and six years later to 601 Merton. Its supply exhausted, its site under pressure for housing, the Davis pottery closed its doors for good in 1931.

This early Davisville house still stands across from the site of Davis' pottery.

Lacking everything which a settlement required in order to grow, like water power, a main intersection and a railway, Davisville remained just a hamlet. And it remained that way longer than most of Yonge Street's other hamlets, for the land that surrounded the crossroads was a "glebe", or clergy reserve, and was never sold off to farmers. Even with the arrival of the street railway, and the incorporation of Davisville and Eglinton as a village in 1889, those lands remained in the hands of the church until 1911 when they were finally sold to developer A.G. Dinnick. Dinnick designed an attractively planned subdivision, with streets radiating from a circular ground that contained a church. But the War interrupted his plans, and the lands remained largely undeveloped until the 1920s. Then, Davisville caught up with the housing boom that had preceded it both to the north and south.

A surprising number of Davisville's old structures have survived, despite the hamlet's small size. Much of this is due to its position as a commercial backwater relative to the major developments that have taken place at St. Clair and Yonge to the south, and at Eglinton and Yonge a short distance north.

Although the pottery itself has long gone, a park called the Pottery Playground marks its last location. Two old houses opposite, at 590 and 592, stand out from the more recently constructed homes, as being clearly from this early industrial period. Davis Villa built by potter John Davis for his son, Alexander, still stands near the northeast corner of Davisville and Mount Pleasant. The home of John Davis himself, originally on Yonge Street opposite Imperial, and built in 1860, was moved in 1908 to 66 Millwood, where it stands yet. And still another Davis family house, that belonging to the youngest son, Joseph, and built originally on the east side of Yonge between Millwood and Belsize, was moved in 1926 just around the corner to 26 Millwood.

Meanwhile, Dinnick's Glebe Manor Estates (so named because the clergy reserve was referred to as a "glebe") remains a stable and attractive housing area. Solid one- and two-storey brick houses line streets that are now shaded by mature trees. The name "Manor Road" is a historical reference to the original scheme.

Sadly, some buildings did not survive. The hotel and the other general store were demolished years ago, and the 1886 church, with its original wooden construction, was razed as recently as 1974, an era of supposedly increasing heritage awareness.

Eglington

Yes, this is how Eglinton was spelled during most of its time as a rural village, and, yes, it was a misspelling. The name comes originally from the estate of the Earl of Eglinton in Ayrshire, Scotland, and was designated in tribute to the many soldiers which Ayrshire provided for the War of 1812. Meanwhile, in the 1820s, a clerical error changed it to "Eglington"— a mistake that lasted until around 1880, even in business directories and municipal documents.

Again, the intersection of Yonge Street with this concession road was the site of an early hotel, which stood on the southwest corner of Yonge and Montgomery. One of Canada's most

John Oulcott's handsome hotel was an Eglinton village landmark standing from 1881 until the 1930s when it was demolished. The North Toronto town hall is visible beyond it.

famous hotels, this was Montgomery's Tavern, where William Lyon MacKenzie and John Rolph launched the Rebellion of 1837 against the dogmatic Lieutenant Governor, Sir Francis Bond Head, and the ruling Family Compact. Here, on December 4, 1837, 800 rebels, determined to bring representative government to Ontario, marched out into the bitter night air and down Yonge Street to Toronto. But lying in wait, near what is now Yonge and Maitland, were Sheriff William Jarvis and 27 riflemen. After only a few shots, the rebels took flight and the rebellion was over. In retaliation, Bond Head ordered the hotel burned, and two of the Rebel supporters — Lount and Mathews — hanged, while MacKenzie fled to the U.S. Far from futile, the Rebellion, both in Ontario and Quebec, led to the government reforms of the Durham Report in 1841 and ultimately to today's system of local government. Rebuilt in 1858, the hotel burned again in 1881, after which John Oulcott built on the site a fine three-storey brick hotel, the Oulcott Hotel. It lasted until the 1930s, serving as a post office during the Depression years, and much photographed, until it was demolished.

Through the 1860s and 70s Eglington could count a Methodist church, blacksmith, wagonmaker, and at least a cou-

67

ple of general stores — Taylor's and Joseph Hargrave's. The area's first attempt at urban development, a plan in 1857 to subdivide the estate of the famed Jesse Ketchum, was ahead of good public transportation, and failed. In 1885 Hargrave obtained the post office for the location calling it correctly "Eglinton". When Eglinton and Davisville incorporated as a village in 1882, the first town fathers built for themselves a two-and-a-half-storey town hall, a handsome brick building beside the Oulcott Hotel. It was also demolished in the 1930s to make way for a police station which stands on the site today.

Like most of Eglinton's village buildings, the old post office is still gone.

By the turn of the century, development was making its way up Yonge Street hard on the heels of the street railway. In 1912, the village of Eglinton, by then the town of North Toronto, was annexed to the City of Toronto. Of Eglinton's early village buildings, only the Hargrave store on Yonge south of Keewatin survives and today houses Wayne's Wine World. A plaque in front of the post office describes the old Montgomery Tavern.

Bedford Park

Near today's Lawrence Avenue, Yonge Street came to a branch of the Don River. A site with water usually attracted more than the usual number of businesses and this one was no exception. In fact, as early as 1804, when Yonge Street was frequently impassable, the Kendrick and the Ketchum families took up their land grants on this section of Yonge. Jesse and Seneca Ketchum began operating a general store from their log cabin, which was located on the south side of today's St. Germaine. Shortly thereafter, in 1829, the Lawrence family arrived and took up their land on the northeast corner of Yonge and Lawrence, while Jacob Lawrence opened a tannery on the southwest corner.

Like all good Yonge Street villages, this one had to have a tavern, and in this case it was James Nightingale's "Durham Ox". It stood on the west side of Yonge at Bedford Park, while Charlie McBride's Bedford Park Hotel stood nearby at Fairlawn. John and James Russell operated a popular general store, until it was taken over by John Atkinson in 1898 and moved to Bedford Park and Yonge where the store still stands.

Bedford Park remained a village out there in farm country until 1890, the year of the boom. In that year, the Metropolitan Street Railway extended its service to the top of Hogg's Hollow Hill, and brought with it the usual land speculation. The biggest development was the subdivision of the Ellis family estate into 1,500 lots. The original plan called for a company town of 1,500 workers' houses built around a factory. The proposal, however, was too populist for a council interested in attracting only the gentry, and it was rejected in favour of more upscale housing. In that year too, Bedford Park joined with Eglinton and Davisville to form the Town of North Toronto.

Despite a slow-down during the First World War, development came swiftly, and Bedford Park was, like Eglinton and Davisville, swallowed. The Bedford Park area has generally been spared the next layer of development, which saw places like Deer Park and Eglinton lose their 1920s townscape to highrises. Rather, much of Bedford Park's early 20th century townscape has endured, and among it, a few pieces of the old village as well. Besides the Atkinson store, there is the home of N.S. Dinnick, developer of the Lawrence Park Estates and brother to A.N. Dinnick of Glebe Manor fame. Built in the 1870s and originally at 3415 Yonge, it has stood at the southwest corner of Teddington and Yonge since 1930. Unfortunately, the Ellis estate house was torn down for a Roman Catholic school.

York Mills

Yonge Street's next village stood only a short distance further on, and although having endured many name changes, is still identified by its early name, York Mills. Unlike the other villages further south, and north for that matter, York Mills had enough water power to attract mills. The first was a sawmill erected by Sam Heron on the east side of the valley. His mill gave the place its first name, Heron Bridge. After Thomas Arnold added his mill in 1817, the place became Millford Mills, and by the time Cornelius van Nostrand had added another in 1844, it had acquired a post office (1836) with the name York Mills.

But there was still another unofficial name to go. In 1850, tavern owner James Hogg decided to try his hand at land speculation and divided his property into village lots. But because of poor public transportation, his scheme flopped, yet the place took on the name of Hoggs Hollow, one still used to this day.

Yonge Street itself had changed a few times. When Jones and his Rangers first came through the area, building the street, they detoured around the steep hill and flood plain, and followed the east wall of the valley. A few years later it was straightened to go directly through the valley, and it was on this alignment that Van Nostrand added a general store and James Hogg a tavern.

The community developed in two sections, the first clustered around the mills on the valley bottom, while part way up the north hill, streets were laid out with workers' houses, a blacksmith, a shoemaker and George Harrison's hotel. Overlooking the entire area is one of Toronto's oldest churches, St. James Anglican, built on Ridge Road, on the east rim of the valley. A pioneer footpath leads to the valley floor in front of it, and remains a well-trodden and popular pathway.

Partly because new development is prohibited in a flood plain, and partly because Yonge took a few deviations, a fair bit of old York Mills can still be traced, streets and buildings alike. The most evident is Hogg's old tavern, now the Jolly Miller, more than 135 years old. For a time during the Prohibition years, it became popular with gambling aficionados, and was the victim of several police raids. When it regained a liquor licence it changed its name. Van Nostrand's store, which stood beside it is long gone. However, from the tavern, Mill Street yet leads to an intersection with "Old Yonge Street" evoking the old townscape. Here, where Donino Street crosses the river, was the site of the Heron mill that got the place started.

Unfortunately, on the northern heights of the village, the redevelopment of the 1970's took away many early homes. Only two workers' cabins were saved, and have been incorporated into the Auberge du Pommier restaurant at 4150 Yonge St.

Lansing

It is hard to believe, looking at the new overwhelming skyline of North York's city centre, that any history could survive in those long shadows. Here, near the intersection of Yonge and Sheppard Avenue, are towering offices, condominiums, a city centre and the new Ford Theatre of the Performing Arts, making it the most important road intersection in that city. This is a role not unlike that enjoyed by the intersection way back in 1805 when the area's first settlers were just beginning to make their way up a muddy and stump-strewn trail known as Yonge Street. The crossroads gained in importance due to the Shepard Mills located a short distance west.

Elihu Pease added a tannery on the southeast corner, while in 1857 Joseph Shepard II opened a store on the northwest corner. This building, two stories high with a wrap around porch and yellow brick trim was operated by the Dempsey family from 1921 until 1989, and was arguably Yonge Street's best known landmark in North York.

As along most of that route, taverns were often the first order of the day, and this was no exception. Here on the corners were John Emerson's hotel and Thomas Hill's tavern. In 1824 Thomas Sheppard built the Golden Lion Hotel, a two-storey building with wrap-around verandah, and a lion carved in oak above the door. This popular watering hole was also a meeting place for those plotting the 1837 Rebellion. The leader in this area was John Gibson.

Lansing remained a small oasis of activity surrounded by fields and pastures. The arrival of the electric street railway

Long a Lansing landmark, the historic Dempsey store at Sheppard and Yonge defied the urban onslaught until 1995 when it was moved.

replaced the plodding stages and brought with it land speculation and new stores. By the time of the First World War Lansing had been swallowed by Toronto's northward advance.

Then, during the 1970s and 80s, another phase swept through the area. North York's dynamic mayor, Mel Lastman, was determined to give his new city the skyline he felt one of Canada's largest cities deserved. In short order, towers were shooting skyward. Yet, in their shadows, a surprising amount of history has survived.

The Dempsey store stood until 1995 when it was moved around the corner onto Beecroft Street. Elihu Peases's house has also managed to survive and stand at 34 Avondale just around the corner from its original Yonge Street location. Two of the Shepard houses have survived as well. That built by Michael Shepard in 1851, and a solid two-storey brick building, following his return from jail for his role in the 1837 Rebellion. It stands in the York Cemetery, about one quarter mile back from Yonge Street. Meanwhile, Joseph Shepard's house, a smaller wooden affair, stands nearby at 90 Berriedale.

Although the Golden Lion Hotel was demolished in 1928, its best known icon, the lion carving, was rescued, and can be seen today in another North York hostelry, the Novotel Hotel in the city centre.

72

Willowdale

More history awaits in the village that went by the name of Willowdale. "Then we came to Willowdale" recounts a writer in the York County atlas of 1878, "where resided Mr. David Gibson whose house was destroyed in 1837 by government troops. He was for a time representative in parliament of North York... A road ran eastward to a famous camp meeting ground on the land of Jacob Cummer where congregated Indians as well as white, to engage in Divine Service."

Originally known as Kummer's Settlement (the original German spelling of the Cummer name) the area was pioneered by Jacob Cummer and his six sons. Their first business, besides the family farm, was a farm implement shop. Devoutly religious, Cummer held Lutheran services in his log house. Later, after converting to Methodism, he held traditional camp meetings on his lands, a portion of which he set aside for a church. His son, Joshua, operated a shingle mill and tinsmith until the business burned in 1865.

Another, and ultimately more prominent, member of the community was David Gibson. An early settler and surveyor, Gibson was exiled for his part in MacKenzie's rebellion. When he returned in 1849, he built a magnificent Georgian mansion on the west side of Yonge Street. Nearby was Ludwig Lehman's store and post office.

The homes of both these prominent families have managed to withstand the onslaught of North York's urban re-advance. Jacob Cummer's home stands at 44 Beardmore, and dates from 1850, while that of Joshua Cummer, built in 1845, stands on McKee Ave. But the area's heritage claim to fame is the Gibson House. Although hidden from view from Yonge Street by a shoddy parking lot, it has been restored to its 1851 period and is now a museum.

Newtonbrook

The difficulty that travellers faced trying to inch their way along Yonge Street is evidenced by the taverns that appeared every mile. The next settlement weary travellers would encounter on their northward trek was Newtonbrook. Unlike the other communities, named usually after the first tavern owner or postmaster, this one was named after Isaac Newton; a democratic decision made by the local population in 1863. Another Cummer was at work here, operating a general store, along with Sam McBride. The place went on to attract shoemakers, millers, tailors, a wagonmaker, and, at nearby Steele's Corners, John Steele's tavern.

Despite the arrival of the stores and housing subdivisions during street railway days, and the redevelopment of recent years (although at a more modest scale than that at Willowdale and Lansing) much of Newtonbrook is still there to see. The former general store is now a donut shop at the northwest corner of Yonge and Drewry (built in 1907). Further west along Drewry is the original Newtonbrook school, built in 1878 and now a religious facility. Just west of the school stands a string of older houses, most of which predate World War Two.

Steele's hotel, the last version built in 1847, became a hunting clubhouse and

About the only thing the same in these photos of Newtonbrook taken a half century apart, is the old corner store – now a donut shop.

tea room and was then moved around the corner where it stood until at least 1954. In all three communities, Lansing, Willowdale, and Newtonbrook, heritage street signs mark the location of these early pioneer places.

Langstaff

Between Newtonbrook and Langstaff, the last of Yonge Street's lost villages, lies the upscale community of Thornhill. Here history lives, as many of this historic place's streets and buildings have been lovingly protected against "heritage-challenged" developers. Hotels, and shops still stand on Yonge Street as they have for a century and a half, while Colborne Street and John Street, with their trees and picket fences, are a trip to the past.

Langstaff, on the other hand, not very big to begin with, has pretty well vanished. It was named after John Langstaff, a teacher who arrived in 1808. His family operated a store, shingle factory and pail factory all situated at the northeast corner of Yonge and Langstaff. In 1870 Langstaff finally earned a post office which was placed in the Langstaffs' woollen mill. Up until then the mail had been delivered on a sled pulled by a dog named Bull.

In addition to the Langstaff family businesses, Andrew Home operated a general store, while a blacksmith shop stood nearby. Strangely, the directories do not list any taverns for this location, an oddity in that it was the first toll gate north of Hoggs Hollow, and such places usually were marked by a watering hole or two. For many decades the name Langstaff was associated with the Langstaff Jail Farm which operated from 1911 until 1976.

The Auto Era has swept aside all evidence of this community. Here the widening of Yonge Street, the building of Highway 7, a four-lane roadway, and more recently the arrival of Highway 407, have left no room for history. Except for a solitary house at 39 Langstaff Road East (built around 1840-1860 and somewhat altered) only the name lives on in "Old Langstaff Road" and the Langstaff commuter railway station.

Dundas Street

4.

The Governor's Road

"The Governor's Road", two centuries ago, was a derogatory term for a boulder-strewn trail that was supposed to be the all-important military road to London. As governor of Upper Canada, Simcoe had two main jobs, to settle the place, and to keep it safe from the military minded Yanks polishing their muskets just across the lake. His Dundas highway was supposed to do both.

As a military route, it was to be kept inland, and link the head of Lake Ontario with London, then proposed as the capital for Upper Canada. From London, the link lay along the Thames to Lake St Clair. But it was also designed to allow settlers into the forests of the territory, and grants were routinely handed to whomever wanted them (although the best, and the biggest went to war heros and influential officers)

The route was to lead from Cootes Paradise — now Dundas — to the forks on the Thames where London was to be located, and eastward to the garrison at Fort York. In 1794 Simcoe assigned his trusty surveyor Augustus Jones to the job. And so with a crew of 100, Jones began to hack his way through the forest. As they slashed away the forest, they encountered rattlesnakes which they killed, although they saved at least a couple to show the governor's wife who noted in her now famous diary, that they hissed when she poked them with a stick. They also encountered numerous wild grapes which, again according to Lady Simcoe, they made into "tolerable wine."

In less than a month Jones had finished the 80-mile survey. But of the road itself, there was little progress. When Simcoe decided to locate the capital at Toronto instead of London, the urgency for the London Section dwindled, and, with few settlers to maintain it, "The Governor's Road" remained little more than a trail through the forest. In fact, a quarter century would pass before the road was open enough to allow stage travel. By contrast, the Toronto section began to attract settlers almost from the start.

But even then travel was tediously slow, and taverns were needed at intervals of six to seven miles to provide rest for the weary teams, and respite for the jostled passengers. Many of these taverns became the focus for hamlets and villages along the route. If there was water power as well, the location was likely to became a centre of pioneer industry.

At that time Dundas Street began at Lot Street, near what would now be the intersection of Queen and Ossington. It led north to modern Dundas Street and then wound its way westward to follow the route of what would eventually become Highway 5.

Following the historic route today is more than a trip into Ontario's past. It also offers a cross section of urban Ontario, from the ancient taverns of Queen Street, through the early 20th-century development that followed the street railways, and then finally to the suburbs of the Auto Age, and the fringes of urban growth.

Blue Bell Village

It's a name that hasn't been uttered by anyone, save the occasional historian, for more than a century, and appears only in dusty volumes on Toronto's history. Yet a century and half ago, it was the destination for "city dwellers" seeking the bucolic country air of rural Ontario. And it marked the start of "The Governor's Road".

In the 1840s, the intersection where Lot Street met Dundas, (now Queen and Ossington) was a long way into the country. Here were clustered a handful of houses and a pair of taverns. The Queen's Head, on the northwest corner, was a small, frame two-storey building with an attractive wrap-around verandah. In front stood a pump for the large horse trough.

Today's intersection of Queen and Ossington marked the location of "Blue Bell" village, the historic terminus of Dundas Street.

Slurping from that trough were the steeds of those who lived in the city to the east, and who travelled to the summer resort atmosphere that the Queens Head offered.

Nearby and a little to the east along Queen, lay another small-frame tavern, the Blue Bell. To emphasize that name there stood a pole with a sign that swung on it to represent a bell. It was from this watering hole that the hamlet took its unofficial name.

The place was also well known for the nearby estates of "York's" more prominent early citizens. One belonged to Colonel Givens, a well-decorated War of 1812 veteran, which he had built as early as 1798. The house was demolished a century later. The other, east of the Givens lands, was that of Colonel Alexander Shaw, another prominent military man. Built around 1794, it consisted of a large log dwelling. North of Blue Bell Village, where Dundas swung west, were the lands of Lieutenant Colonel Richard Lippincott Denison, one among a well known early Toronto family dynasty. Before the arrival of the railways in the 1850s - 70s, the only industry in the area were market gardens, the produce from which was sold at Toronto's St. Lawrence market.

By the 1870s, the Blue Bell Tavern was gone, and the name fell from use. But because Queen Street was the main route, not just to Dundas, but to Lakeshore Road, it became a main axis for Toronto's growth. By the 1870s two railway lines passed close by and a string of stores, houses and businesses soon lined Queen Street. Engulfed by Toronto's urban sweep, Blue Bell Village had lost not just its name but its distinctiveness as a rural village. So thorough was the inundation that nearly all evidence of Blue Bell Village has gone. Even the street names, Lot and Dundas, are now Queen and Ossington. The only reminder is a later tavern at the northwest corner that now goes by "Gondoratu"

Brockton

One of the ways designed to pay for the upkeep of roads like Dundas was the hated toll gate. The first along Dundas was that at Brockton, roughly where Dundas and Lansdowne are today. Here, where Dundas was "little better than bush," three hotels clustered east of the toll gate. This trio of taverns, Collard's Hotel, Joe Church's Brown Bear, and the "Queen Street" Hotel were nicknamed the "Appii Forum". At the barrier itself was John Mullon's hotel where teams of horses and wagons travelling to and from Hamilton were often lined up. Ferlin's general store contained the area's first post office known originally as "Lippincott". It was later renamed Brockton to honour Sir Isaac Brock, fallen hero of the 1812 War.

Like many Dundas Street villages, Brockton developed around a toll-gate and taverns.

The community boomed in 1840 with the arrival of Irish immigrants fleeing the devastating potato famines decimating their native island. Many of them found work in Mullon's farm or in one of his abattoirs (located on St Clarens north of Dundas). The heart of the village became the intersection of Dundas and Brockton Road (now Brock Avenue), where a small string of labourers' cabins acquired the nickname of "Stoney Butler Village."

But as with Blue Bell Village, the urban frontier was not far off, and in 1882 street car service had made its way to Brockton's eastern limit (Dufferin Street). The village, claiming it had nearly 750 residents, was populous enough to become incorporated, and in 1881 commissioned a town hall on the southwest corner of Dundas and Brock. Three years later it was annexed by Toronto. By 1893 electric streetcar service arrived, turning the heads of those used to no other form of transport than by horse.

With the new means of travel, stores began to compete for space along Dundas, and the farm fields behind them were sub-divided into streets and housing lots. By the end of the century Brockton, like Blue Bell, was another Toronto suburb.

But unlike Blue Bell, there are a few buildings that linger amid the later development. For example, the rooflines on the buildings at 1603-05 Dundas reflect an architectural style that predates the urban onslaught and most of the commercial structures that stand today. Although not architecturally striking, the old town hall still stands, while the street signs carry heritage markers proclaiming them to be those of "Brockton Village 1881".

Seedbed of Canadian Nationalism

The War of 1812 is considered by some historians to be the "seedbed of Canadian nationalism" because of the complete military victory over the Americans, and because it was the first concerted "Canadian" war effort. Among the heroes were General Isaac Brock and Lt. Colonel Henry Proctor, who were instrumental in staving off the superior American invasion force. The war ended, with no loss of Canadian territory, with the signing of the Treaty of Ghent in December of 1814.

Lambton Mills

From Brockton, Dundas swung north to meet another important farm concession road, today's "Bloor Street." Here, a hotel and small collection of buildings huddled about the second toll gate, and, a short distance north, the old Peacock Tavern, although the place seems never to have acquired either a post office or a name of any kind. Then, after passing through more farms and forest, Dundas arrived at the first major obstacle on its route, the Humber River.

For a few years, Dundas detoured down to the King's Mill to cross the river. However, Dundas Street itself acquired a bridge in 1816, and mills appeared there as well. The first was a saw and grist mill built by York innkeeper, William Cooper. In 1845 William Pearce Howland took over Cooper's old mill and replaced it with a five storey frame flour mill which could put out an unheard of 150 barrels of flour a day. Across from the mill he added a store and post office, and behind that his house. Next to it stood a handsome brick tavern with a wide, decorative verandah: the Lambton House Tavern.

On the western bank of the river Thomas Fisher built a four-storey mill, part wood and part stone. It burned in 1844 and Fisher replaced it with another that was all stone to the third storey. Fire broke out again in 1902, and despite a desperate dash by the Brockton fire department, the mill was again destroyed.

The trend to convert mills to restaurants or hotels is not a recent phenomenon. In 1910 Howland's mill had become the Lambton Mills Inn with dining room and concert hall. But hotels are as flammable as mills, this one falling to flames in 1915, taking Howland's store with it. In 1923, Lambton Mills finally acquired its own fire brigade.

Because of its water power, Lambton Mills became busier than most of Dundas Street's other villages. By 1846 with a population of 250, it could claim besides the mills, three taverns, two stores, two blacksmiths, two wagonmakers and a distillery. The Credit Valley Railway appeared on the scene in the 1870s and added a station a short distance away.

Howland's mill at Lambton Mills served as a restaurant before burning down in 1915.

Lambton Mills remained a rural retreat until after the First World War. Street cars began service to the area, turning at the Lambton Tavern (where, it is said, conductors would instruct the drivers to turn the vehicle slowly enough to allow a quick libation). In 1928, a high-level bridge replaced the narrow iron bridge and urban growth spread over the fields.

Thanks to the presence of a lovely riverside park and an informative booklet by the Etobicoke Historical Board, Lambton Mills offers much to see and to explore. On the east side of the Humber, "Old Dundas" runs from Varsity Avenue to the river. Although towering apartments and rows of town-houses have overwhelmed any ambience of the early village here, tucked at their feet stands the still elegant Lambton House Tavern, as of this writing undergoing restoration.

On the west side, a few metres of Old Dundas retain the rural appearance of a narrow, tree-lined side street down to the river. From this point, Humber Boulevard, a seasonal one way road, follows the bank of the river through parkland, right down to the Old Mill at Bloor. On the way it passes the vague foundations of the Fisher Mill, located near the public washroom.

83

Almost out of place in a forest of high rises, the old Lambton House tavern is being restored.

Kingsway Crescent, winding and tree-lined, leads south from Old Dundas and represents another early route to the Kings Mill. Although most of the housing now in the area dates from the 1920s building boom, while others date from the 1960s and 70s, a few early houses from Lambton Mills' village era stand out. Look for a clutch of them on Kingsway Crescent just south of Government Road, and a pair located west of that on Government Road itself.

Sadly, modern Dundas Street itself was not so fortunate. The expansion of the road to four lanes and the compulsion to surround every heritage structure along it with a parking lot, has obliterated any heritage ambience the historic road might otherwise have had.

Islington

Although Dundas Street here crossed Mimico Creek, there was insufficient water power to attract any significant mills. Instead, a small settlement grew up around the intersection of Dundas Street with Burnhamthorpe Road, then a pioneer path which allowed settlers northwest of Dundas to bring their grain to the mills on the Humber River. On the hill overlooking the creek Thomas Montgomery in the 1830s built a large stone tavern; by the road junction itself, the Islington House was added in 1839.

Half a dozen years earlier Thomas Wilcox had opened a store with the area's first post office and its first name — Mimico. That all changed in 1858 when the name "Islington" was chosen after a neighbourhood in London, England. A Methodist church was added in 1843, replaced with a brick structure in 1887.

During these years of difficult road travel, the farmers were further frustrated by the difficulty in getting to the mills which were about a mile south of Dundas. At this time Islington Avenue did not cross the Mimico Creek. To help them get access, Montgomery built a road across his property connecting Dundas with Bloor, the concession road which led to the mills. In 1846 William Smith counted two sawmills, a blacksmith, two shoemakers, as well as wagonmakers and tradesmen of various skills. Its population was estimated at 150.

In 1879 the railway came to town. Although the Great Western had laid its rails to the south along the lakeshore in 1856, and the Grand Trunk to the north through Weston about the same time, Islington had to wait nearly 25 years until the Credit Valley Railway added its rails to Ontario's spider web of rail lines. Although its impact was not as telling as that of the earlier lines on the communities through which they passed, the railway did add some impetus to the village's economy. The station was built near Islington Avenue southeast of the village core. Because Islington Avenue was cut at the creek, the road to the station followed today's Cordova. The original Credit Valley Railway station was replaced around the turn of the century with one of the CPR's new station styles.

Although the mills on the Humber gradually began to shut down, or more likely, burn down, farmers could still turn to the railways to ship their produce, and the village remained a busy rural community. It retained its rural flavour until after the Second World War when the Auto Era ushered in a building boom. In the 1960s Dundas and Islington were widened to four lanes and large sprawling shopping centres began to replace the neighbourhood stores as the place to shop. The CPR removed its pretty, little wooden station about this time as well. Shortly afterwards the TTC opened its Islington subway station a half mile south, and the landscape changed dramatically once again. With suddenly improved access to the city, commuters began to demand rental housing, and they got it, as apartment towers began to pierce the sky.

Once more, thanks to an Etobicoke Historical Board booklet, the heritage of Islington is easy to find. Burnhamthorpe Road was bent south to meet Dundas at a new junction west of its original intersection, the latter now marked by Burnhamthorpe Crescent. Between the two corners, there yet stands the old Hopkins store, now much altered and home to the Lily chinese restaurant. The H.M. Watch Repair and Robert Hair Styling together occupy the parsonage of the 1887 church, now gone. Surprisingly, the earlier 1843 church survives, buried within the Precinct Restaurant, named to commemorate a brief stint as a police precinct. Sadly, the old Islington Hotel, which lasted nearly a century and a half, was demolished in 1986 to make way for a nondescript cookie cutter style Citibank. One of the village's grander homes, the Thomas Musson house, is now the Antique Shoppe. But the jewel of the community is Montgomery's Inn. There it stands, on the southeast corner of Islington and Dundas, restored and land-

One of the Toronto area's most significant historic buildings, Montgomery's Inn is now a tea room and home to the Etobicoke archives.

scaped and now home to a tea room, to community meetings, and to the Etobicoke Historical Board which has done so much to preserve and celebrate the heritage of a community. Behind it, Montgomery Road still directs traffic southeast to Bloor, as it has for more than 150 years.

Despite efforts of a modern streetscape to denegrate it with strip malls and endless traffic, Montgomery's Inn stands out as one of the Toronto area's most attractive and important "lost villages" buildings.

Summerville

After modern Dundas crosses over Highway 427, it becomes six lanes of roaring traffic. A stream of cars and trucks turn to enter motels, big box stores and fast food restaurants. But 170 years ago, farmers clucked their teams north from Dundas, down Mill Street to the Silverthorne grist mill. They might first have stopped at the store which stood on the northeast corner to do their shopping, or later, when post offices began to open, pick up their mail.

The community was founded by John Silverthorne who arrived from Niagara-on-the-Lake in the early 1800s and looked carefully for a place to build a mill. Here, where Dundas Street crossed the Etobicoke River, he chose a bend in the river, a perfect place for a milldam and pond. He then added a short street, which was called Mill Road, to link Dundas with his saw and grist mills. As settlement along Dundas boomed, the community added a blacksmith, hotel and various tradesmen. Mrs. McCourtney and William Hivell operated general stores, while the Credit Valley Railway put up a small shed-sized flag stop. But by the end of the century the mill was gone, followed eventually by the entire village. Today there is not even an original street name to indicate that this once vital pioneer community ever existed. Mill Road is now known as Silvercreek Road, and contains only modern, industrial buildings and warehouses. Most drivers do not even notice the creek over which they cross.

The Heart of Dixie

Although it was little more than a mud track, Simcoe's Dundas Highway began to attract settlers almost from the beginning. Many of them, after all, had received the land free, as a reward for their military service. However, it was not until the government erected a hated toll booth at the corner of what is today's Cawthra Road, that the nucleus of a village began to appear. Since they had to stop anyway, the travellers reasoned, why not have a drink? And so taverns appeared here, too, along with churches and then a general store and post office. It was not called Dixie right away. It suffered through such names as Fountain Hill, Sydenham and even Oniontown, before it was eventually called Dixie, after Dr. Beaumont Dixie, a local landowner who had donated land for the chapel.

Worship at first took place in William Cody's tavern, until Cody helped build the community's first chapel, the Union Chapel, in 1816. Settlers would come in and stomp the snow off their boots in the little log building. In 1837 the growing community replaced it with a more substantial stone chapel. Amazingly, this simple but solid structure has withstood the ravages of time and redevelopment, and survives yet. If the name "Cody" rings a bell, one William "Buffalo Bill" Cody, founder of "Buffalo Bill's Wild West Show" south of the border, was baptised in the Dixie Union chapel.

Unlike Summerville, Dixie is a small oasis of history. Although three of the hamlet's four corners have been buried beneath the asphalt, the northeast corner contains not only the little Dixie chapel, but the Dixie Presbyterian Church, built in the early 20th century to the north, and St. John the Baptist Anglican church, a handsome, spired brick church to the east. Surrounding it is the treed cemetery which contains graves dating back to 1812. Here linger some small fields, an old orchard and an early village house, all of which will likely disappear over the next few years. Until then, Dixie will remain a pioneer island deep in the heart of suburbia, bombarded by a ceaseless roar of traffic on Dundas' six lanes, and overwhelmed by the area's commercial overkill of strip malls and mega stores.

Dixie Union Chapel, where the legendary "Buffalo Bill" Cody was baptized, stands watch over busy Dundas Street.

Cooksville

More often than not, the intersection of two important pioneer roads became the site of pioneer businesses and institutions. The road built from the busy harbour of Port Credit on Lake Ontario to meet the Dundas Highway was no exception. Because the lake was still Ontario's only reliable "highway" the intersection became a busy one, with Daniel Harris' general store being one of the first to locate there. In 1818 the road from the lake was extended further north, and in 1848 reached the top of Georgian Bay to become a settlement road known as Hurontario Street, a name that it retains to this day. During the early years of its life, the intersection carried the name "Harrisville", after the store owner. Meanwhile, Jacob Cook, who had been busy operating the local stagecoach, decided in 1829 to open a tavern and seven years later the name was changed to Cooksville.

Besides being simply a crossroads intersection, albeit a busy one, Cooksville also acquired a brickyard, a railway station on the Credit Valley Railway, and a role as the administrative centre for the township of Toronto.

But things began to change as early as 1929. In that year the Dundas Highway was widened to four lanes. A decade later North America's first limited access highway, the Queen

89

Elizabeth Way, was completed and urban expansion began to head Cooksville's way. As post war sprawl gobbled up the farmlands around Cooksville, the place lost its identity as a village, and became just another set of stoplights on a pair of suburb traffic arteries. The only historic crossroads structure of note to survive is the 1860 general store, now shared by Irwins Hardware, and the African Caribbean Groceries. It sits just east of the historic crossroads on the south side.

On the northwest corner, another old store is occupied by Optical Plus, while a few early '20s-type shops have managed to survive on the north side of Dundas, west of the lights. Beyond the intersection lie Cooksville's old streets, but most of the simple wooden homes that once graced them have gone.

Springfield

While the name might not spring immediately to mind for area residents, the name Erindale will. Although Dundas Street had been open for nearly three decades, the land along the Credit River belonged to the Mississauga Indians until 1820, when the government persuaded the group to part with it. Just two years later, land speculator Thomas Racey hustled in to open a 38-acre townsite. Within three years the place had became a busy village with a church, store, tavern and, thanks to the waters of the fast-flowing Credit River, several mills. It's first name was Toronto. However, because two other places would end up using that name as well - York and Port Hope the name of Springfield was officially adopted.

Springfield's boom years lasted until 1853 when the Great Western Railway opened its Toronto Hamilton branch along the lakeshore, too far away for the town to benefit. In 1879 the Credit Valley Railway placed a station in the town, but the trend had already shifted to the lakeshore. In 1890, the name changed once more, becoming Erindale, after the English estate of the Anglican church's first minister, James McGrath. (In 1904, the farm which occupied his Canadian estate, Price's, was the first in Canada to produce pasteurized milk!)

Being a little further from the source of urban sprawl than

Cooksville or Dixie, Erindale did not lose its separate identity until the 1960s and 70s. And it hasn't entirely lost it even now. On the eastern wall of the wide Credit River Valley, and south of Dundas, are the old village streets with names like Jarvis, Robinson and Proudfoot. They are still pleasantly narrow and lined with trees. However, most of the early wooden homes have been replaced with larger 1960s style houses.

Back out at the corner of Jarvis and Dundas, the earliest buildings to survive include the 1877 Methodist church and the rectory built in 1861 for the previous church building. East of the rectory on the south side of Dundas, a few earlier buildings yet line the historic route. However, when the highway was widened in 1948, bypassing part of the original road, those which lined the north side were removed. Dundas Crescent marks that old route, while the steep winding trail that once twisted into the valley and past the mills has been replaced by a high-level bridge, and the mill sites are now occupied by a park and new businesses.

Across the valley on the west wall, dominating the entire scene as it has for over a century, is the church of St. Peter's. With its soaring spire, it was built in 1875 on the site of a church that was started in 1825. The cemetery behind it contains grave markers that date back to that early period. Just a block west of the church, strangely out of place in its suburban setting, is one of the oldest buildings on Dundas Street. There, on a large lot, and surrounded by stately maples, is "The Grange". Built as a summer home for Ontario Chief Justice John Beverly Robinson in 1833, it takes its name from Toronto's historic "Grange" built in 1817 for Robinsons's brother-in-law, D'Arcy Boulton. Thanks to the far sightednesss of the development firm of Cadillac Fairview, who acquired the property for development, "The Grange" now belongs to the City of Mississauga, and is the building used by the Boy Scouts.

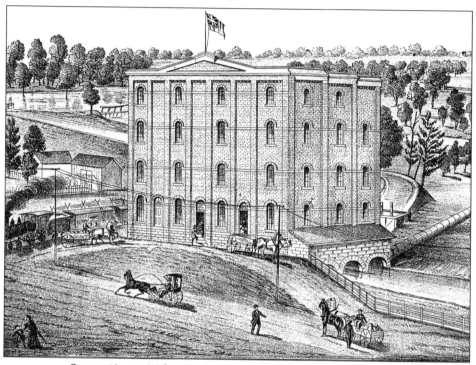

SPINK MILLS, W. & J. SPINK PROP'S, DUFFINS CREEK, ONT.
MANUFACTURING CAPACITY 250 BBLS. PER DAY.

5.

The Lost Villages of The Pioneer Kingston Road

Governor Simcoe's successor, Peter Russell, was clearly worried. "The isolated situation of York surrounded by water or unsettled country," he explained to the legislature, "makes me anxious to open roads with as little delay as possible." The assembly, huddled in the drafty wooden buildings by the bay, agreed, and ordered Russell to find a "great highway throughout the province." Fortuitously, on March 26, 1799, a settler appeared before the executive council. His name was Asa Danforth, a Yankee who had recently arrived at the capital of Newcastle District, a now vanished village called Presqu'ile, on the Bay of Quinte. For $90 a mile, he offered to build a road for them which would connect York with Presqu'ile. The council bought the idea, and instructed Danforth to clear a road 33 feet wide, 16 and a half feet of which was to be smooth and "cut even to the ground." And it was to be completed by July 1, 1800.

June 5, 1799, bugs swarming about their heads, Danforth and his crew began hacking their way eastward from the east bank of the Don River. His progress was rapid at first and by July 26 he had made good headway through Scarborough and Pickering. But the winter slowed his progress, and by May of 1800 he was pleading for an extension.

The quality of his work was already coming under harsh criticism. "I regard it to be a good winter road," remarked William Chewitt, acting surveyor general, "but with regard to a summer road, nothing can affect that but a good settlement thereon." Danforth himself agreed, for only settlers on site could maintain the road. "Fifty or sixty persons should be put on the land without delay," he argued. However, the executive council had already doled out much of the land in large blocks to influential (but absentee) government officers, and along 63 miles of road, there were only four settlers.

With no one to maintain it, the road quickly became impassable. The council accused Danforth of not fulfilling his obligations, and Danforth stomped off back to the U.S., thoroughly disgusted. Through Scarborough, Danforth's road followed a circuitous route. Rather than staying close to the lake, where settlers were likely to take up land, his route angled inland far to the north of the lake. To protest the lack of roads, a pair of lake side settlers, William Cornell and Levi Annis, decided to build their own road to connect with Danforth's. From their holdings, at the foot of today's Markham Road, they cut their trail westward, meeting the Danforth Road roughly at today's Victoria Park Avenue, a route at first called the "Cornell Road". Then in 1814, buckling to pressure, the legislative assembly voted funds to straighten and improve the road. By 1817, it was open to Kingston, and renamed the Kingston Road.

From its junction with the Danforth Road on the west and to Highland Creek on the east, the Kingston Road was straighter and closer to the lake. However, east of that point, it followed Danforth's road for much of the way to Brighton. Through Scarborough, Danforth's road can be traced, west to east, along the modern roads of Clonmore, Danforth Road, Painted Post Road, the Colonel Danforth Trail and Military Trail. But in only a few places, such as north of the intersection with St. Clair, are any early buildings evident.

The original Kingston Road followed today's King Street east from Parliament Street as it first angles northeast to join Queen Street before crossing the Don River. On his way, the pioneer would pass

By the late 1800s, Kingston Road had been much "improved".

94

Little Trinity Church, behind it the Enoch Turner school, both dating from the middle of the last century. The pioneer path then continued east along what is now Queen Street to the junction with today's Kingston Road at the site of the former Greenwood Racetrack. The route then winds up the hill east of Woodbine Avenue and with another hill east of Birchmount Road, to mount the heights of Scarborough.

The Greenwood Racetrack was closed in 1994 and is now slated for demolition. It was originally called Woodbine, but was renamed when the new Woodbine Racetrack was built in 1956.

In the West Hill area, new and old Kingston Road separate; the old descending into the valley of Highland Creek, and out again, the new becoming the forerunner of today's Highway 401.

An interesting and long-abandoned segment of Cornell's original road follows a public path down the hill at the foot of Hill Crescent, which is a southward extension of Bellamy Road. Only wide enough for a wagon, it still displays the ruts dug into its dirt roadbed by early pioneer stagecoaches. Some local historians claim that vague foundations on the flats at the bottom of the hill are those of a long forgotten hotel.

Although stage travel commenced in 1817, Kingston Road remained a mess, with, according to one disgruntled traveller, "deep inky holes which almost swallowed up the four wheels of our waggon." Twice-weekly service began in 1830 with the legendary William Weller advertising new carriages and an "improved" road, but even he could average only a tedious two to three miles per hour.

In 1835 a Scottish road engineer named John McAdam devised what seemed to weary travellers a dream come true: a smooth road. By layering the road surface with 10 inches of crushed stone, the highway would, if properly done, maintain a level surface. To this day the technique is called "McAdamizing". The trustees of the Kingston Road, however, scorned the high cost, which they put at 4,000 pounds per mile, and opted instead for the much cheaper technique of planking the road at 500 pounds per mile. To pay for the improvements they placed toll houses at intervals along the way at Norway (Kingston Road and Woodbine) and at Scarborough Post Office (Kingston Road and Eglinton). But the planks quickly deteriorated, to no one's surprise, and the private road company went broke. Shortly after, the newly formed County of York was obliged to take over the maintenance of the Kingston Road. By this time, however, the Grand Trunk Railway was being built and would soon reduce long-distance road travel to a trickle.

Leslieville

At the foot of today's Berkeley Street (originally called Parliament Street) in Parliament Square, stood Ontario's first crude legislature building. The road to the east then continued along what is today King Street to where it joins Queen crossing the Don River, then treelined, on a narrow, wooden bridge, where it encountered the Don Mount toll house at today's Broadview Avenue. In those times, with a simple hotel on one corner, and Scadding's log house a short distance north, Broadview was called "Scadding" south of Kingston Road, and the "Don Mills Road" north of it.

Although it was a solid brick house, the Leslie family house, located on Queen Street (then called Kingston Road) has not survived.

A survivor from Leslieville's last days as a distinct hamlet is the Duke of York Hotel, still standing on Queen near Leslie.

Kingston Road then led through forest and fields to the spacious nurseries of John Leslie that marked the fringe of the village of Leslieville. Taking up 20 acres of grant land, Leslie established a nursery, and in 1852 opened a post office on the corner of what is today Queen and Curzon. Growth clustered around this intersection with the opening of a hotel by George Smith and William Cook called "Uncle Tom's Cabin." It was replaced in 1870 by the more substantial brick Morin House, which stands to this day as the Duke of York Hotel.

Thanks to a thick layer of fine clays that lay beneath the topsoil, Leslieville became the centre of an active brickmaking industry. Among the first were James Russell, who opened his operation in 1857, followed by David Wagstaff in 1863. By 1870 the business directories were listing nine such yards, some of which grew to be among Canada's largest. But the clays were soon depleted, and housing was built over the yards. Remnants of one of the last of these yards stood by the CN railway tracks at Greenwood until the 1970s, when they were also buried beneath more houses. The only reminder of that early and vital industry in Leslieville is the home of brickmaker James Price, still standing at 100 Greenwood Ave.

Leslieville's other businesses included a piggery (the site of Leslie Street school), a slaughter house (on today's Curzon) and a general store with a post office that opened in 1852. In 1856 the Grand Trunk Railway added a station that stood at the level crossing with Kingston Road, on the south side of the road and east of the tracks. By the turn of the century it had been replaced by a larger and fancier building, more in keeping with the urban land boom then engulfing the area. A turreted brick station, it stood north of Queen on Degrassi Street. After surviving the demise of its railway role for some years as a retail outlet, CN finally demolished it in the early 1970s.

But Leslieville's most historic landmark was not a building, but a tree. Just south of Queen on a small street called Laing stands an enormous red maple tree. It was this magnificent specimen that inspired Alexander Muir to compose the still moving song The Maple Leaf Forever. The "Maple Cabin" in which he briefly lived, along with a plaque, identify the location.

With the extension of streetcar service east of the Don River in 1887, urban growth quickly overtook the village and the farms, and made Kingston Road, by then called by its new name, Queen Street, an urban arm of a booming Toronto. In 1884, Toronto annexed the area, allowing the extension of water and sewer services.

Norway

Queen Street was still called Kingston Road and was still a dirt path when in 1793 Sarah Ashbridge a widow from Philadelphia, moved to the area and gave the name to the bay whose waters once extended right to the roadway. Still surrounded by large grounds, the handsome Ashbridge house (built in 1854) yet exudes a rural ambiance that is otherwise lost along this once rural road.

From the Ashbridge Estate Kingston Road turned northeastward. Here the Woodbine Hotel sat, tucked into the angle formed by Kingston Road and an easterly extension then known as Maple Avenue (now Queen Street). Kingston Road

When the beautiful Ashbridge house was built in 1854, Queen Street was a dusty country road.

then entered the village of Norway. Known originally as Benlamond, Norway developed around another of those infuriating toll houses. James Smith, the toll keeper, also had time to operate a store and the Norway House Hotel. Much of the village's early activity centred around the Norway steam mills which began operation in 1835. Another early business involved a boarding house and store operated by Frank Boston, an immigrant form Yorkshire England, at the corner of Kingston Road and Benlamond (now Main), where the community of Benlamond was centred. From this intersection, a pioneer path known as the Dawes Road angled northeastward to the community of Wexford.

Ira Bates moved in from Scarborough and took over the Norway House, while Daniel Sullivan operated a hotel halfway up the hill to the Banlamond Hotel, a rise of land known as Mount Sullivan. On the south side of Kingston Road, nearer to Woodbine, was the Woodruff House which provided area farmers with a market in which to sell their produce. When Boston's hotel burned in 1881, he replaced it with a bakery, which over the years remained a popular landmark in east-end Toronto.

For a time the Lains Lumber Company operated here, processing pine hauled in from as far away as Scarborough. William Brotherson was for years the village smithy, while Charles Ferguson and J. Hodgins ran general stores, which, along with Crew's post office, were popular gathering spots for the villagers. Among the things they no doubt argued over was the coming of the new streetcars; an intrusion which, as in Leslieville, would bring the urban growth that obliterated the community as a distinct and separate rural village.

It did a pretty good job of it, too, for not much remains of the original village. Hotels and early houses are all gone, although the historic post office lasted until 1982 (on the northeast corner of Kingston and Woodbine) when the Ontario Municipal Board rejected pleas from the area's heritage supporters and allowed the building to be demolished. A mere five years later the Benlamond Hotel was torn down, and shortly after that, Sullivan's hotel suffered the same insensitive fate. The corner's most prominent landmark is the St. John's Norway Cemetery, with the village's only remaining early structure, the St. John's Norway Church, constructed in 1893.

Mortlake and the Famous Halfway House

Kingston Road continues east from Main, tracing its original route past several blocks of stores that date from the arrival of streetcar service. Along the way are the exclusive Toronto Hunt Club, which once boasted its own private streetcar siding, and Fallingbrook, the site of the former home of famed railway builder, Donald Mann. In Blantyre Park, just east of Fallingbrook Road, is the historic but little known junction of Colonel Danforth's road and the successor, Kingston Road. While Kingston Road heads off on its eastern alignment, Clonmore Avenue angles northeast to the busy CN railway line. Prior to the rails, it continued on to join today's Danforth Road at its junction with Danforth Avenue immediately north of the tracks.

East of Birchmount Avenue the landscape changes once more, with more modern suburban housing dominating. As

Kingston Road's famous pioneer "Halfway House" was a popular gathering spot for travellers. It now rests at Black Creek Pioneer Village.

the route mounts another hill to reach the heights of Scarborough, it passes the site of another early hostelry, the White Castle Inn, where the name lives on in a modern hotel. But arguably the best known of the old Kingston Road hotels was the Halfway House located on the northwest corner of what is today Kingston Road and Midland.

Built in 1850 by James McClure, it marked the halfway point between Dunbarton and York, a day's journey by stage (and what sometimes still seems like a day's journey in heavy rush-hour traffic). In 1865 Alexander Thompson opened a post office in the building, and gave it the name Mortlake. Nearly 40 years later, the Toronto and Scarborough Electric Railway extended their line along Kingston Road and located a waiting room in the old hotel. It remained a popular gathering spot for touring bicycle clubs and local community groups. But the Auto Era put an end to all that, and the handsome old hotel deteriorated, losing its magnificent verandah, and finally becoming a local convenience store. In 1965, the Metro Region Conservation Authority came to the rescue, purchasing the building for $1000 and moving it to Black Creek Pioneer Village, where it has been restored as a stage stop for

101

Kingston Road's radial roadway days are relived on this mural near St. Clair. The building depicted on it is Scarborough Collegiate Institute, now R.H. King Academy.

the village visitors. Here they can relive Kingston Road's early days by munching down a ploughman's lunch in the old tap room, or a more substantial meal in the new basement restaurant. Meanwhile, back on Kingston Road, an outdoor mural beside the original site depicts pioneer days at the hotel.

A legacy of the street-railway days is the system of identifying the car stop with numbers. To this day long-time Scarberians still refer to this intersection as "Stop 14", and that at St. Clair as "Stop 17", where a local store incorporates the old number in its sign.

While Kingston Road offered more than a half dozen hotels between the Norway and West Hill toll houses, such as that owned by Jonathan Gates at Bellamy Road and Kingston Road, none attained the celebrity of the old Halfway House.

Scarborough Post Office

This hamlet was at first centred around Kingston Road's intersection with Eglinton Avenue, then a narrow dirt farm road. Here, on the highest point on the Scarborough portion of the Kingston Road, stood a general store, with its all-important

102

post office, the Washington Methodist Church, and Levi Annis's Inn. Methodist services were held in the tavern until 1838 when a new church was built on land donated by Annis, using money donated by Stephen Washington. In appreciation the church was named "Washington". In 1856, when the Grand Trunk Railway was forced inland from its lakeside alignment to bypass this height of land, "Scarborough" moved to trackside a mile west near the modern-day intersection of Markham Road and Eglinton Avenue, and was renamed Scarborough Village. Doomed to stagnate, the old hamlet was finally swept away in the suburban boom of the 1950s. A new church occupies the crest of the hill, with the original church bell as a memorial.

Across the six-lane road, a string of large apartment buildings stand where the store and a few houses once stood. The only building that dates from the hamlet's early days is the stone farmhouse on the northeast corner of Kingston Road and Scarborough Gulf Club Road, now a popular pub named Casey O'Gills. This is the fine, stone farmhouse built in 1867 by Jeremiah Annis, a descendent of one of Scarborough's founding families. A short distance west of Eglinton's current intersection with Kingston Road is the homestead of William Cornell, the instigator of Kingston Road. Built in 1836 it survives, much altered, surrounded even now by fields.

Highland Creek and West Hill

Contrary to the usual trend of village amalgamation, these two communities, still separate communities today, began as one, Highland Creek.

This location enjoyed benefits that other communities between here and York did not. Here, the old Danforth Road rejoined Kingston Road after rambling through northern Scarborough. Highland Creek offered a water course that powered the early mills as well as providing a shallow channel for boats to the lake, an encouragement to early settlement in a day when roads were, if they even existed, impassable.

One of those early settlers was William Knowles, who arrived

103

in 1802 and established a blacksmith business. His son Daniel opened the first general store, and helped found the Markham and Pickering Wharf Company, which shipped farm produce and lumber from Port Union to U.S. ports on Lake Ontario.

The valley of Highland Creek is narrow and steep, and communities developed on both sides, with churches, stores and other village businesses. Hotels were kept by William Keeler, while William Morrish, M. and M. Byrne and F.C. Kirkham at various times operated general stores. Down in the busy valley, T.C Kirkham ran a woollen mill and James Maxwell a flour mill. Maps produced in 1860 showed a total of four mills at this location.

In 1804, Cornell journeyed to Kingston to get his mill stones and built Highland Creek's first mill. In 1847, Thomas Helliwell, whose family started the first mills on the Don River at Todmorden, added a grist mill on the south side of Kingston Road on the site of Cornell's earlier mill, which had been consumed by fire. But in 1880 fire razed this one as well. He later built a chopping and cider mill.

Highland Creek even enjoyed a flurry of oil speculation in the 1860s. Hoping for a boom like that being enjoyed in the

Highland Creek is another early Kingston Road community where history survives, mostly in its elegant outdoor murals.

104

The historic Richardson house, still standing on Old Kingston Road in West Hill.

famous Lambton oil fields, 150 speculators poured $25 each into an oil drilling company and crossed their fingers as the drills started turning, their optimism buoyed by occasional showings of the black goop. Unknown to them, however, a local prankster was clandestinely pouring oil into the rig during the night, and the only true deposit proved to be salt.

In 1879 John Richardson opened a post office on the west side of the valley and gave it the name West Hill. West Hill extended west from the top of the Highland Creek valley to modern day Morningside. It included a small "suburb" of shanties, built by Irish railway workers in the 1850s and called Corktown. In 1906 the radial railway extended streetcar service to the location, and the face of the village began to change. In the 1920s improvements to the Kingston Road brought more growth. In 1936, "new" Kingston Road was built to bypass the valley and subsequent road widening and redevelopment removed most of the early village buildings between Morningside and old Kingston Road — the Shackleton Hotel and carpenter shop, Pritchard's post office, and several houses. Then in the 1950s and 60s, the post-war suburban boom swept over both places, spurred on by the opening of the Highway

401 bypass in 1958 just a short distance east.

Nevertheless, a handful of old buildings on early village side streets give a partial glimpse into those village days. On Old Kingston Road, just east of its junction with "new" Kingston Road are the old village streets of Manse Road and West Hill Crescent. A guide, prepared by the Scarborough Historical Society, points out the old Melville Church, built in 1852, and the later manse opposite it. On the southwest corner of Old Kingston Road and West Hill Drive stands the house of John Richardson, whose son, John Hunter Richardson, opened West Hill's first post office. The son's home and the former post office are immediately to the west. On the north side of Old Kingston Road stands the Queen Anne style home of Sam Heron, one the area's first settlers.

Further west, on new Kingston Road, stand a couple of structures that also belong to West Hill. These include St. Margaret's Church, built in 1906 to replace an 1833 structure, which was the first Anglican Church east of the Don River. The other is the former Durnford store, now a pub on new Kingston Road, just west of the lights at Old Kingston Road.

Heritage-wise, the village of Highland Creek did not fare as well. Most of its original commercial core was replaced with 1960s style commercial strip development, although a couple of the buildings sport outdoor murals with historic themes. In the cemetery, which contains some the area's earliest burials, only a plaque commemorates the original church. However, about a mile east, although still considered a part of Highland Creek, on the northwest corner of Kingston Road and Meadowvale stands the handsome (former) Morrish general store. This large, brick building, which yet retains its fine verandah, was built in 1891, had 15 rooms and even boasted an elevator. The Morrish family operated the business until 1967. Sadly, the building is now vacant and boarded.

Meanwhile, down in the valley, the mills had disappeared by 1900. Since then, floods and park landscaping have removed all traces of them.

106

Rouge Hill

East of the Highway 401 overpass, the streetscape of Kingston Road changes once more. Back on its original alignment, Kingston Road is six lanes wide, and lined with suburban sprawl and strip development. Mere metres away more traffic roars along the 12 lanes of the 401, a total of 18 lanes of non-stop traffic, leaving little room for heritage.

Highway 401 is a mere 50 years old. Opened in 1956-7 and designed to handle 48,000 cars a day, it was carrying twice that number in two years, clogging the four lanes at just 15 miles an hour.

Much of that heritage was linked with the Rouge River which Kingston Road crossed a short distance further east. Once a busy prehistoric portage to Lake Simcoe, the Rouge was the site of native settlements long before the Europeans arrived. While Kingston Road remained a muddy quagmire, the swampy mouth of the river harboured an intermittent boat building industry. Two vessels reportedly built at the Rouge River "shipyards" were the schooner Duke of York commissioned by Captain Hadley in 1820, supposedly one of the fastest on the lake, and the Canada by a Captain Henderson. A third and final vessel was built in 1843.

On the eastern summit of the steep valley wall the hamlet of Rouge Hill developed. It began as a stage stop with hotels operated by Thomas Holborne and Hugh Graham. Farmers urged their teams down the Altoona road from the farmlands of northern Pickering Township, pausing here at their favourite watering hole, before carrying on to the mills on the Rouge, or to the wharfs at Dunbarton. However, the hamlet remained small, and when the arrival of the Grand Trunk Railway in 1856 killed off much stage travel, the site became a backwater. By 1860 there was no longer any evidence of the old mills. Today, the six lanes soar across the valley on a high-level bridge, while three early structures survive. On the south side, facing the now dead end Altoona Road (cut off by the 401) are a pair of the hamlet's houses, although well-hidden by trees. A third house stands on the northwest corner, an attractive gothic-style dwelling.

107

Dunbarton

Once an important village, Dunbarton, too, has all but been swept away; first by the new CN railway line and then by the ever-widening Kingston Road.

The history of Dunbarton is decidedly different from those of Kingston Road's other early places. Unlike the stage stops which gave rise to other villages, Dunbarton traces its start to the presence of Frenchman's Bay's harbour. In 1832, William Dunbar, hoping to take advantage of the proximity of the bay to Kingston Road, laid out a townsite and called the location Pickering Harbour. He dredged through the sandbar which cut off the bay from the lake, and added wharves at the north end, near the fledgling village. However, the site proved too shallow and silt-laden to be profitable, and the wharf facilities were relocated closer to the channel, to be named Fairport.

William Dunbar's old village, however, did not entirely wither away. When the Grand Trunk Railway arrived, their line came close enough to the village to warrant a station. In 1890, the business directories indicated that the village contained at least a blacksmith and a couple of general stores, which served an estimated population of 150.

This Dunbarton general store, still standing, is a typical example of those which existed more than 100 years ago.

The 1960s brought with them not just suburban boom times, but the building of a new railway line, linking CN's main line (the former Grand Trunk) with its new container yards northwest of Toronto. The rails ripped right through the western end of Dunbarton, severing the main street and removing a number of its early structures. Today's Kingston Road was bent to bypass the site, inadvertently saving the town's historic core from oblivion. The former Kingston Road is now just a local road (renamed Dunbarton Road), and remains narrow and quiet. In the centre of the village, at the corner of Dunbarton Road and Dunchurch, one-time general store still stands, along with a former hotel and a brick blacksmith shop. Stretching along the south side of Dunbarton, and for a short distance south on Dunchurch, until it is cut off by the 401, is a string of early village houses, some dating back to the 1840s and 1850s. Meanwhile, dominating the village from its spacious perch on the north side is the magnificent Dunbar Mansion.

Liverpool

Also known as Liverpool Market, this small crossroads hamlet sprang into existence when Fairport replaced Dunbarton as the area's main port. Here, where the road from Fairport met Kingston Road, there appeared a large hotel with a short-lived post office in it. Because it was only one half mile from Dunbarton, it gained few other businesses. When the Grand Trunk arrived, Fairport declined, as did the need for Liverpool Market. Amazingly, however, the handsome old hotel has withstood the ravages of suburban redevelopment and, a few metres back from its original site, carries on the time-honoured crossroads tradition— it is a restaurant and bar called, naturally enough, the "Old Liverpool House."

Built in 1850, this odd-looking residence housed the practices of Doctors Burns and Tucker. It still stands on Old Kingston Road in Pickering.

109

Duffins Creek

Like Highland Creek, Duffins Creek had a number of geographical advantages. It had water power, to allow for the development of mills, and it gained a railway station when the Grand Trunk arrived in 1856. It all began when an early Quaker settler named Timothy Roger arrived in 1812 to establish a Quaker Community. He chose the site wisely — on a main stage route, where Sam Munger had opened a hotel seven years earlier, close to shipping and mill sites. On one of those sites he built the area's first sawmill.

More mills and taverns began to locate here as well. Head's mill was built in 1837, and the Sparks mill, a landmark for many decades, was built in 1875. Among the taverns were those operated by Leonard, Whiteside and O'Leary. Early directories noted that Duffins Creek contained several churches, a school-

Duffins Creek became Pickering at the turn of the century.

house, a brewery, and a station on the Grand Trunk "at which all trains stop". The early, wooden station was busy enough to be replaced in the 1890s by a larger, brick station of typical Grand Trunk design, which stood until the 1960s.

The streets of Duffins Creek included the "old" Kingston Road, the "new" Kingston Road, Church Street as the main north-south artery, and Mill Street. Thanks to the dedicated work of the local LACAC, and the historical society, much of old Duffins Creek is saved and celebrated. A walking tour map leads along "old" Kingston Road and through the old village centre. Along the street are a pair of 1890s stores, and two doctor's houses, one built in 1871 for Dr. Byron Field by his father, the other, sporting a couple of copper cupolas, was built in 1850. It housed the practices of Dr. Burns and Dr. Tucker from 1860 to 1880. Nearby are Head's Hotel, dating from 1850, converted to a store in 1874 and renamed the Dale Block, and "Gordon's Hotel", built in 1881 by John Cuthbert.

An interesting intruder is the "Courtyard" Mall. It represents an effort to complement the history of the old town with an architectural style somewhat more reminiscent of medieval Europe. Gone now are the mill and, not surprisingly, the railway station. The urban fringe which has swallowed all Kingston Road's villages to this point has only arrived in recent years, but the efforts to preserve old Duffins Creek in advance of this onslaught will mean that here is a village not doomed to vanish utterly.

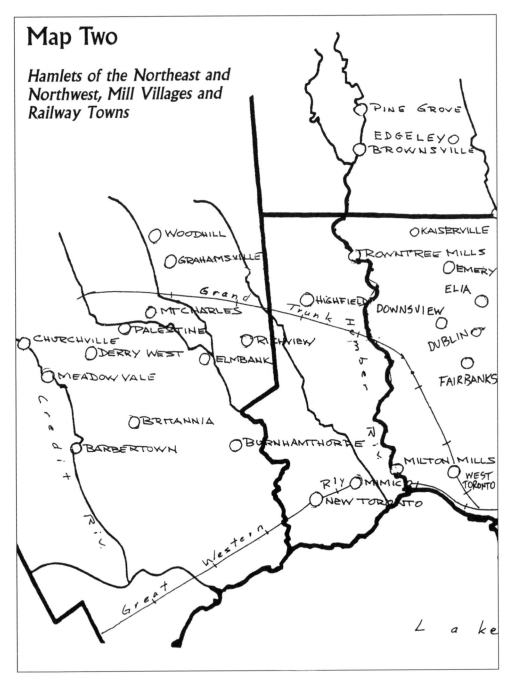

Map Two

Hamlets of the Northeast and Northwest, Mill Villages and Railway Towns

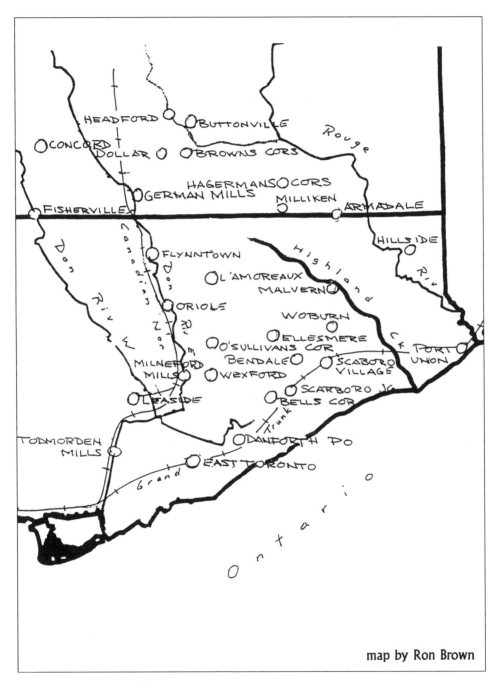

map by Ron Brown

O'Sullivan Corners

6.

⌒

Vanished Farm Hamlets of Scarborough and the Northeast

In 1996, the City Scarborough celebrated its 200th anniversary. Two hundred years earlier, when the township was surveyed, it was a land of forests, ravines, and of course, breathtaking bluffs. These yellow cliffs of clay and sand inspired the wife of Ontario's first governor, John Graves Simcoe, to name the area after the chalk cliffs of Scarborough England. In 1804 Asa Danforth hacked through the undergrowth to lay out his winding "Danforth Road to Kingston", a path so tortuous that it was quickly replaced with a straighter Kingston Road.

Still, settlers remained few. David and Mary Thomson were the first, struggling in 1799 to assemble their crude log cabin on the banks of the Highland Creek beside a now-forgotten trail to Markham, itself the site of a flurry of clearing by Berczy's German settlers. Over the next 20 years a small settlement grew up around their cabin and became known as St. Andrews. As early as 1804 William Cornell built the first mill several miles to the east, near the mouth of the Rouge River, but by 1820 the population of the township remained less than 500.

Transportation remained the problem. Roads were quagmires at best, where stage drivers felt lucky to make a dozen miles a day. Taverns abounded on the Kingston and Markham Roads as rest and respite for weary teams, and wearier passengers. As stage drivers were usually rewarded by tavern owners for halting at their establishments, such rest stops were often longer and more frequent than necessary.

Then in the 1820s, and again in the 1840s, what had been a trickle of European immigration turned into a flood. Wealthy

115

landowners in Ireland and Scotland were driving out peasant farmers through starvation and land consolidation, and many made their way to the growing town of York. The fertile soils of Scarborough were close by and the population tripled in just 30 years.

Scarborough's early road pattern was typical of an Ontario farming township. In addition to the pioneer roads of Danforth and Kingston Road, and a now-vanished early route of Markham Road, Scarborough's roads were laid out in a grid pattern. The roads which ran east-west were called concession roads, and it was along these that the farm lots were surveyed. These concession roads, like St. Clair, Eglinton, Lawrence and Ellesmere, were about a mile and a quarter apart. The north-south roads were the side roads, like Kennedy, Brimley, Bellamy and Warden and were about three quarters of a mile apart.

Before the automobile, travel was tediously slow. Roads were often quagmires, and scarcely passable. Farmers needed every-thing close at hand — the stores where they could shop and, more importantly, pick up their mail, blacksmith shops and harness shops, churches for worship, and taverns for recre-ation. And so, at most of the important intersections, cross-roads hamlets appeared containing these vital services.

Up until the Second World War, the township was one of Ontario's most prosperous farming areas. Fields of grain waved in the breeze, while cattle grazed lazily in lush green pastures. Farm houses of brick or stone lined the dirt concession roads, behind them the sturdy barns. Cars soon clattered along, rais-ing clouds of dust and startling the teams that still plodded along dragging their creaking hay wagons across the fields. Distant whistles and columns of smoke heralded another train with its line of red box cars or green passenger coaches. But with the end of the War and the advent of the Fifties, the idyll would vanish forever.

Although it was due to open at the same time as the Queen Elizabeth Way, in 1939, the 401 bypass was delayed by the War and not completed until 1955. But the effects of the Auto Age were already being felt. The closeness to the burgeoning city of

Toronto, which had until then been a boon to the farming community, would now signal its demise. With the car craze came the suburbs. Unplanned at first, many just appeared wherever the speculators wanted them, regardless of whether the municipal necessities of sewers and roads existed or not. Mills, houses and hotels came tumbling down to make way for the endless rows of backsplits and sprawling industries, while many of the old crossroads hamlets have long been replaced by donut shops and adult video stores, and the mill sites cleared away for parkland or housing. The once tranquil farm lanes were widened and paved to welcome in the Auto Age.

To anyone braving these six-lane traffic tunnels, where strip malls stretch to the horizon, the place seems entirely bereft of any history at all. Yet, thanks to groups like the Scarborough Museum and the Historical Society, there remain small islands of history — an ancient church surrounded by tall trees and toppling tombstones, a few quiet one-time village streets, a handsome, old stone house — surviving in this sea of suburbia.

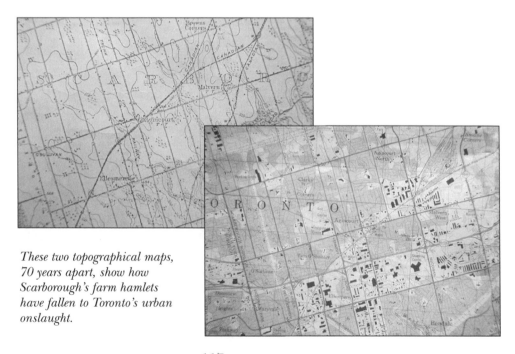

These two topographical maps, 70 years apart, show how Scarborough's farm hamlets have fallen to Toronto's urban onslaught.

117

Danforth Post Office

Opened by Asa Danforth in 1799, Danforth Road was poorly built and fell into disuse. By 1801 Kingston Road had replaced it. The trail, however, carried on in use as a local farm road, providing access into northern Scarborough from its junction point with Kingston Road near Victoria Park Avenue. Various local streets follow much of that alignment through Scarborough — Clonmore, Danforth Road, Painted Post and Military Trail.

Roads like St. Clair and Warden were laid out originally as concession roads or side roads to give frontage to the farms then being sold to hopeful pioneers.

At the intersection of Danforth Road and Birchmount Avenue (as it is known today) a small post office was opened on the property of an individual named Brown on the southeast corner of the intersection. A short distance east, a school stood on the south side of Danforth, while a trio of farmhouses clustered about the crossroads. Today, Danforth is four lanes wide and commercial development has taken over the intersection.

Bell's Corners

While the name Scarborough Junction pertains more to the junction of the Nipissing Railway with the Grand Trunk (GT) in 1873, a short distance east, a busy crossroads settlement had already grown up here. Known as Bell's Corners, this was the junction of three roads: St. Clair, Kennedy and Danforth. The Farmer's Inn was located at the intersection of Kennedy Road and Danforth Road, while the general store operated by Bell was located at the northwest corner of Kennedy and St. Clair. To the north of that stood Emp's blacksmith shop.

In 1856 the Grand Trunk built its Montreal line a half mile east of the intersection, but in 1873 when the Nipissing Railway chose the area for its junction point with the GT, the community boomed. A townsite was created and new stores and houses appeared (see chapter on railway towns).

Laurel Avenue was one of Scarborough Junction's early streets. The houses here have been replaced or surrounded by urban expansion.

Today, Danforth Road, now four lanes wide, still follows much of its earlier alignment. Indeed, three early farm homes can still be seen on the north side of Danforth Road between St. Clair and Midland, while the early Hunter store still sits on the south side close to St. Clair (vacant at the time of this writing).

On the northwest and northeast sides of the Kennedy and St. Clair corner, a cemetery and gas station have replaced the store and shops, as has a gas station at the northeast corner of St. Clair and Danforth.

Bendale

Bendale represents Scarborough's most historic site, the place where settlement began. Here, where an early version of Markham Road wound its way northeastward, David Thomson and his brother Andrew erected their crude shanties. The year was 1797. Yonge Street was only a year old, and Asa Danforth had yet to clear the dense forests for his road east. It was a particularly difficult time to be trying to locate and clear land in what was then a daunting forest.

The community at first went by the name of Benlomond and was centred on Danforth Road and Lawrence. However, that name was also used for a community near Norway on the Kingston Road, and, when it came time to find a name for the post office, Bendale was chosen.

The community was more a scattered rural community rather than a concentrated village. A short distance from the Thomsons, John Wheler constructed a sawmill on the west side of Brimley and south of Ellesmere, and shortly thereafter a grist mill. The grist mill burned down in 1863.

In the 1840s, the Thomson brothers' sons built new houses, James building the house he called "Springfield" east of the family homestead, and William adding "Bonese" to the west. Between the two, the community added a handsome brick church, beside which a library building was added in the 1890s. A quiet farm road twisted its way past the Thomsons and the church connecting Brimley and McCowan. During this period, the Thomson family controlled most of the farmland between Kennedy and Brimley, and between Lawrence and Ellesmere. The Canadian Northern laid its rail line across the Thomson land, but surprisingly, never added a staion.

The suburban tide rolled through this area during the 1960s. Remarkably, it spared much of Bendale. This preservation victory is due to the foresight of the hardworking members of the Scarborough Historical Society, who managed to save the church, the library building and both Thompson houses. All stand today on St. Andrews Road, and are celebrated with historic plaques. The road itself has retained much of its early characteristics, narrow and winding as it passes through the woodland that yet surrounds the old church, a miniature landscape from the past.

"Springfield" has been designated as a heritage structure, and holds roots for such Canadian luminaries as Lord Thomson of Fleet, and Farley Mowat. Further west, where St. Andrews meets Brimley, the elegant stone Bonese is also designated "historic".

On the south bank of Highland Creek is the Scarborough museum with a pioneer log cabin and the 1858 Cornell family farm house. Even a portion of the long-abandoned Canadian Northern right of way has become a footpath through the park. Meanwhile, closer to Ellesmere, the Wheler house has also been saved, and is now part of the Bendale Bible Chapel.

Woburn

Woburn's place in the history of the municipality of Scarborough goes beyond the few buildings that constituted the long-vanished hamlet. Here at the intersection of the old Danforth Road, and the Markham Road, an earlier pioneer, Thomas Dowswell built a tavern and called it the Central Inn. In 1850, Scarborough, like many other townships in Ontario, was granted municipal status. Finally, decisions that affected the township could be made by the township's own residents. All they needed was a place to meet. Because Dowswell's tavern stood in the middle of the township, the first councillors began to meet there. The original name of Elderslie was rejected as the name for the new post office because another Elderslie existed in Grey county. Instead, it was named after Woburn, Dowswell's home town in England.

Soon afterward a township hall was erected and saw many heated council sessions in the chambers. In 1922 the office was relocated to the area of Kingston Road and Birchmount, an area then just beginning to feel the pincers of Toronto's urban growth. Back up at Woburn, the old hall burned in 1927, while Dowswell's hotel lasted into the 1960s when it was demolished to make way for look-alike suburban growth. The old Danforth Road is now called Painted Post Road, and is a residential street. Today only a plaque marks the spot where Scarborough began.

Come rain, sleet or snow...

The Romans with good roads and fast horses, could virtually guarantee next-day message delivery within a range of 280 kilometres or so. In the early 19th-century, in comparison, a letter mailed from Quebec City to Windsor, Ontario took about ten days. The Grand Trunk Railway greatly improved Canadian postal service, reducing that delivery time to 49 hours.

Wexford

One year after St. Andrew's Church was built, another church was being constructed on old Dawes Road, an early pioneer wagon road just south of Lawrence. Modelled after the first pastor's home church in England, St. Judes' Anglican Church was described by an early writer as a "perfect gem". Built by local farmers, its style is noticeably different than the traditional symmetrical church structures popping up all across Ontario. On the south side of Lawrence the Catholics added a church while, in 1876, a Methodist church was built some distance to the east, near the corner of today's Birchmount Avenue. It was known as Twaddles' Chapel to honour the farmer who donated the land.

Wexford began, as did many crossroads hamlets, with a tavern. It was around Richard Sylvester's "Rising Sun" tavern that the hamlet with its general store and blacksmith shop grew. Despite the arrival of the Ontario and Quebec Railway, with its small flag station, Wexford remained small, with many of its early buildings along Lawrence between the old Dawes Road and Pharmacy. As the urban growth of the 1960s spilled northward, old Dawes Road was widened and renamed Victoria Park, bringing with it plazas, apartments and housing, sweeping Wexford away.

The little railway station had already gone, having burned in 1933. The buildings that clustered around the crossroads were obliterated. The Catholics replaced their old building with the

St. Jude's church in what was once Wexford still stands on Victoria Park Avenue. It is now engulfed by more modern apartments.

more modern Precious Blood School and church which stands today. Over at Birchmount, the Twaddle Chapel shares ground with a newer structure, as does the "perfect gem", St Judes'. Surrounded by towering apartments, it is set back in a grove of trees, flanked yet by its pioneer cemetery, while a new church building stands to the east.

O'Sullivan's Corners

Close by stood the community of O'Sullivan's Corners, little more than a hotel with a post office in it. It stood at the intersection of what is today "Old Sheppard Avenue", north of Sheppard Avenue's current intersection with Victoria Park. It was started by Patrick O'Sullivan in 1860, and in 1892 added a post office. For many decades the hotel remained a favourite eatery for the area's Sunday drivers. While the hotel was demolished in 1954, an early-style brick farmhouse, engulfed now by modern suburban homes, still stands a short distance west.

L'Amoreaux

Situated at the intersection of Finch and the old Dawes Road, L'Amoreaux was named after a family of settlers who arrived in 1816. Early business surveys in the 19th century show that the authors could not agree on the spelling of the place, as it appeared variously as L'Amoroux and L'Amorioux.

The hamlet grew to include a school, a blacksmith shop, a wagon factory, a sash factory and a couple of churches nearby. On the southwest corner stood James Lang's store with its all-important post office. The blacksmith and wagonmaker stood to the west of it.

This was one of those odd places where two roads, surveyed from opposite directions, did not meet. Victoria Park represents the boundary between the old townships of Scarborough and North York, and each township had a different survey pattern. As a result, North York's Finch Avenue met Victoria Park about half a mile north of where Scarborough's Finch Avenue met it, creating a dogleg for through traffic on Finch. To make

L'Amoreaux's old Methodist church is decidedly out of place on modern Finch Avenue

for a smoother traffic flow, the former has been diverted to meet the latter at Victoria Park.

The old portion of Finch that the new section bypassed has become Pawnee Ave, and is a residential street in a subdivision, with no evidence that it was ever a tranquil farm lane. However, west of a street called Cherokee, there is evidence of a long-abandoned section of old Finch in a park. While most of the old crossroads buildings have vanished, a couple of L'Amoreaux's more important structures still stand, strangely out of place in the sea of suburbia. They include the "little red schoolhouse", now preserved by the City of North York, standing as it has since 1869 on the south side of Finch east of Leslie Street. A short distance further east, and built just four years later, is the brick Zion Methodist church, surrounded by towering apartments, and boarded up, although it is slated for preservation. The graveyard around it contains the stones that commemorate many of those early settlers who would be astonished at how the area had changed.

Hillside

The 19th-century community of Hillside contains one of Ontario's premier tourist attractions, the Metro Zoo. Yet few zoo patrons have likely even heard of the little hamlet. The place began around 1840 with the sawmill operations of William Milne, an industry which outlasted all other Rouge River mills.

Hillside's historic board-and-batten church stands near the forested Rouge Valley in North Scarborough. Its neighbour is the Metro Zoo.

Here his son William A. in 1871 built a handsome homestead he named Hillside. The community was scattered along Finch Avenue between the Rouge and Meadowvale Road, and included a school, church and a number of mill workers' homes.

While newer homes have invaded the wooded hillsides of this riverine area, it has yet to be completely engulfed by the approaching urban tide. Old Finch and Sewell's Road yet wind through the forested valley of the Rouge, much as they have for decades, and cross the river on Toronto's only suspension bridge, a structure that was designed by Frank Barber and completed in 1912 for a mere $8,000. A 1904 descendent of the first school, built around 1853, now serves as a day-care centre, while a solitary village cabin lurks in the woods on the northwest corner of Finch and Meadowvale. But the prize of the area remains the historic board-and-batten church, on the south side of Finch at the intersection of Reesor, a structure that dates from 1877, and remains surrounded by trees and open space. Some distance west, where Finch bends north onto Sewell's Road, the delightful "carpenter gothic" Hillside House stands yet, now saved as part of the Rouge River Provincial Park.

125

Mill owner William Milne's elegant house was named "Hillside", a name that was applied to the hamlet near which it was built.

Hough's Corners

It's hard for anyone carried along by the ceaseless flow of traffic of Eglinton Avenue as it nears Birchmount Road, to believe that this area could ever have been a tranquil dirt trail through farm country. Yet this very intersection, mere decades ago, heard only the sound of horses' hooves hauling hay wagons past fields of blowing grain.

In 1804 John Hough settled in the area and a decade later was operating a sawmill, a wagon shop and blacksmith, all on the southwest corner. A school and church were soon added and the crossroads became a busy farm hamlet. However, following the Second World War, Scarborough Township Council began promoting the area as the Golden Mile of industry, and the farmland vanished beneath sprawling factories. Apartments and houses took over Birchmount and the hamlet has vanished. The only survivor is the cemetery on the east side of Kennedy south of Eglinton.

Ellesmere

The name will be familiar to many, but for the wrong reasons. Today's generation knows it as yet another of those traffic arteries responsible for the usual suburban noise and pollution. In truth, the name derives from the busy farm village that once dominated the intersection of Ellesmere and Kennedy.

In 1820, Archie Glendenning braved the wilds of distant Scarborough to build a general store for the nascent farm community. The place grew slowly and it wasn't until 1853 that a post office was finally permitted in Glendenning's store, which he operated from his fine stone farm house. By then the place could boast two blacksmiths, and two general stores, along with carpenters, jewellers and shoemakers, and a number of houses on the northeast corner. The Forfar (or Forfair) family had three members involved in the hamlet's businesses, including a butcher shop, one of the blacksmith shops, and a wagon factory. The directories of the day estimate the community's population at around 100.

Many of these buildings still stood into the 1960s and 70s when Kennedy Road began to deteriorate into commercial roadside sprawl. Sadly, the historic Glendinning store, built in 1830, was shortsightedly demolished as recently as 1980 to make way for a new, and not very interesting, bank building. All other evidence of this historic community has utterly vanished, replaced by one of Scarborough's more unsightly examples of unplanned urban sprawl.

Modern-day Scarberians will be hard pressed to recognize this hundred-year-old view to be that of the now noisy intersection of Kennedy Road and Ellesmere Avenue.

127

Milliken

Today, this one-time pioneer crossroads hamlet has become the centre of the Toronto area's newest Chinatown which makes it even harder to visualize as a place where farmers cut the ground with horsedrawn plows, and smoke rose sleepily from quiet, rustic houses.

Milliken is situated at the intersection of Kennedy Road and Steeles Avenue. The area's earliest settler was a Loyalist named Norman Milliken who arrived in 1807 and established a sawmill and hotel. Soon after, Ferguson's general store appeared and Henry Boatten took over the hotel. The Toronto Nipissing Railway built a small shelter-sized station to act as a flag stop for the community.

This was another of those dogleg intersections where Scarborough's old Kennedy Road met Steeles about one quarter mile west of where Markham Township's Kennedy Road met it. Most of the hamlet centred around the easternmost of the two corners, and survived more or less intact well into the 1960s, a period when the area was still popular for its market gardens and pick-your-own vegetable farms. It was one of the last in Scarborough to become engulfed in the tide of suburbia, and monster homes and mega malls have replaced the farms.

Only a small string of older village houses survives on the east side of "Old Kennedy" north of Steeles, while a GO commuter station stands on the grounds of the old station flag stop.

Malvern

Malvern was one of those places that had dreams of becoming a thriving village in its own right. But despite a promising start, the railways bypassed it, and it became a backwater, almost an early ghost town.

Markham Road, although less travelled than Kingston Road, was nevertheless a busy pioneer path, linking Kingston Road with the thriving settlement of Markham that the Berczy settlers had founded. Here, at the busy intersection of Markham Road and what was then the Lansing Road that led to Yonge

This 1966 view of Mammoth Hall in Malvern shows that the destructive forces of urban sprawl have yet to arrive.

Street (now Sheppard Avenue), John and Robert Malcolm opened the "Speed the Plough" inn. Its early name was "Brown's Corners" named after the area's first postmaster.

Not content to leave the place just another crossroads hamlet, David Reesor, in 1857, laid out a town plot on the northeast corner, with a half dozen village streets and numerous house lots. But he needed to give it an appealing name if he was to attract buyers. Having heard from locals of a nearby spring which had waters with curative powers, Reesor gave it the name of Malvern, after a place in England which also reputedly had "magic waters".

The place started promisingly enough, adding a church, two stores, two blacksmiths, a wagon shop, Badgerow's woollen factory, and a couple of hotels. But its early promise faltered when the Grand Trunk Railway built its line well to the south. With new businesses flocking to railside, Malvern's growth slowed. Many of the housing lots remained vacant, and the community resigned itself to a role of just another crossroads hamlet.

Hopes were renewed in 1911 when the railway building team of Mackenzie and Mann announced that Malvern would have a station on their new main line to Ottawa, and indeed

129

the station was a handsome, wooden two-storey with operator's living quarters on the second floor. But Ontario did not need three main lines running east from Toronto, and the Canadian Northern Railway failed. It was absorbed by the Canadian National a few years later, and abandoned. By the 1960s, most of Malvern's early functions had finished and the fringe of suburbia crept closer. The Mammoth Hall, with its curling rink and dance hall, remained a landmark until the 1970s. While discussion raged over a possible heritage designation, it became the victim of "heritage lightning," and burned.

However, two of the village homes have managed to survive on Ormerod Street, one of Reesor's village streets. It leads east from Markham Road, just north of Sheppard.

Short-sighted, modern-day developers have chosen to ignore the heritage of the area, and have buried the village site beneath condos and shopping plazas. For David Reesor, that would have been good news, but it came too late.

Armadale

If anything survives in Scarborough's early crossroads hamlets, it is usually the church. This holds true with the vanished hamlet of Armadale. Here, at the intersection of Markham and Steeles, the hamlet contained the usual tavern, blacksmith and general store, as well as a temperance hall and brickyard. The post office opened in 1869 with the unusual name of Magdalla. However, the name was changed to Armadale and stayed that way. The hamlet's first store sat on the southwest corner, another just south of that, with a blacksmith shop behind it. Here too stood a temperance hotel. The Armadale Free Methodist Church was built in 1880, and is now designated under the Ontario Heritage Act. It stands, incongruously surrounded by modern factories, one half mile west of Markham Road on Passmore.

Now a designated heritage site, Armadale's old church is surrounded by a modern industrial park.

130

The hamlet of Hagerman's Corners as it appeared in the 19th century.

Hagerman's Corners

Named after Nicholas Hagerman, one of the early German settlers who accompanied William Berczy into the remote forested lands, Hagerman's Corners is located in Markham Township at the corner of Kennedy Road and Steeles. It contained a hotel, store, shoemaker and two cabinetmakers, and a population estimated at 100.

A church was built by the Hagerman's private burial grounds. William McPherson opened the hamlet's first general store in the 1830s while James Fairless added another in the 1850s. It later became Galloway's and lasted until recent times. The hotel known first as Webber's was taken over by "Tom" Hemmingway and renamed the Beehive with a poem on its sign which read:

131

Within this hive we're much alive
Good liquor makes us funny
So if you're dry, come in and try
the flavour of our honey.

Much of this little community still survived into the 1970s, when the suburban fringe appeared on the horizon and marched into the community. Although the cemetery is still there, the church has long gone, although, about one kilometre west, the former school has been converted into a fine restaurant. Three 1850s homes have withstood the onslaught and stand at 7710 Kennedy, 7505 Kennedy and 7703 Kennedy.

Browns Corners

The traffic today roars through the intersection of Woodbine and Highway 7 looking for turn signals or big-box stores, scarcely aware that there was once a quiet little hamlet at this point, surrounded by fields, and silent save for the clomp of horses' hooves, or the lowing of cattle in the pasture. Yet, on the northeast corner there was a shoemaker, George Feeley, John White's blacksmith shop, Tom Amos' store, and an Orange Hall. On the northwest corner, on the farm of the Brown family, after whom the hamlet was named, John Clark operated a tavern. A blacksmith shop stood on this corner as well. Other businesses on the southwest and southeast corners were a shoemaker, carpenter and another blacksmith. A couple of sawmills operated in the neighbourhood as well.

Most of the intersection today is taken up with turning lanes, and parking lots. The only reminder of the crossroads hamlet is the home of Alex Brown, built in 1850, and now located at 8980 Woodbine Avenue, north of the intersection.

Dollar

West of Brown's Corners, at the intersection of what is today Leslie Street and Highway 7, a little hamlet called Dollar struggled to survive. True to form, it contained a store, post office, blacksmith shop, and church. With railways and main roads bypassing it, it remained a backwater on the landscape, and a footnote in history. In the 1950s Highway 7 was paved, and later widened. Traffic increased and country homes began to appear. In 1972, the northeast corner was cleared of the last three houses for a motel, and for many years the only evidence of the place was the vacant lot on the northwest corner where the store stood. Then the suburban boom struck with a vengeance in the late 1980s and early 90s. Today the roads have been widened even more, the farm fields have become offices and stores, and all memory of Dollar has gone, mostly in the name of the...dollar.

Emery Flag Station

7.

᠎

Vanished Farm Hamlets of the Northwest

Much of the land underlying the urban sprawl of the Greater Toronto Area was prime farmland. No sooner had the surveys for the roads and the farm lots been finished when the settlers began to stream in. Many, at first, were veterans of the wars with the U.S. taking up the land grants that were their reward. Others were Loyalists and refugees from the newly created republic to the south.

Initially, their main route north was Yonge Street, opened in 1796, but scarcely passable. Side roads stabbed east and west from the trail into the dark forests. Many of these were named after early tavern keepers on Yonge Street, such as Steeles, Finch, and Sheppard. But to many the roads were a barrier rather than a convenience, and they sought shorter routes. One such short cut was the Vaughan Road. It originally branched north from Davenport Road near today's Bathurst and angled northwestward until it reached what is today called Dufferin Street, then a farm settlement road, surveyed in a straight line northward into Vaughan Township (hence the name "Vaughan Road").

Despite the efforts of the surveyors, travellers found they had to veer off the line in order to avoid swamps and low-lying valleys beside the west branch of the Don River. In the 1850s, municipalities were created and given the responsibility of maintaining local roads. During that period, the Vaughan Road was straightened and planked and given the name "Gore and Vaughan Plank Road". But this era marked the arrival of the railways, and many municipalities diverted their funds to attract the steel rails, and neglected the roads.

In a belated response, the Ontario Government finally

assumed responsibility for some roads, creating a roads department within the Department of Agriculture.

As it was throughout Ontario, the difficulty of travelling meant farmers needed their facilities close at hand, and many of the intersections in North York and Vaughan sprouted little crossroads hamlets. Nearby streams sometimes afforded enough water power for sawmills and gristmills to operate, but the clearing of the forests frequently dried up the streams, and the mills seldom lasted out the century.

Urban growth began to make its way up Yonge Street during the late 1800s; a trend accelerated by the building of the street railways. By this time, too, urban growth had reached the lower portion of the Vaughan Road, around Bathurst and St. Clair. But the streetcars, which brought stores and subdivisions in their wake, did not make their way up Vaughan Road, and suburban growth there did not really begin until the 1920s. North of Eglinton, despite some scattered rural development, the suburban boom did not arrive until the 1950s.

The rate of urban development significantly increased when the subway was built. Toronto opened its seven-mile long Yonge Street subway line in March of 1954. It was the only one in Canada at the time, beating out Montreal by twelve years.

It then crept steadily northward, reaching the Finch and Steeles areas in the 1960s and 70s, and then invading the lower reaches of Vaughan Township itself in the 1980s and '90s. Still unquenched, developers began moving their bulldozers into the Brampton area in the 1990s, burying history beneath condos and "big box" retail stores.

Sadly, much of this early era in Ontario's rich history has been obliterated by those who put profits first, or who perhaps were just never fully aware of the heritage they were destroying. Thanks to local historical societies, a small number of thoughtful municipal politicians concerned enough to go against the tide, and occasionally a conscientious developer, a few buildings have managed to withstand the tide of suburbia and tell the stories of the heritage that lies in their own backyards.

136

Etoberoba P.O

Fairbanks

Dufferin Street and Eglinton Avenue is as busy as an intersection gets. Cars jam the roads, crowds jostle on the sidewalks displaying an ethnic mix of Italians, West Indians, and Jews. While the area today goes by many local names, Fairbanks is seldom one of them.

To reach the location 170 years ago, settlers like William Moore and Daniel Tiers had to make their way through the dark forests, travelling on rutted roads west from Yonge Street along Eglinton, or northwest on Vaughan Road. Like most, the hamlet of Fairbanks was never more than a local service centre. Thomas MacFarlane's Hotel was probably the most vital of those services, even more so when it acquired the post office in 1877. He had taken over the inn in 1867 from Thomas Gladstone and called it the York and Vaughan Hotel. When it burned in 1870, MacFarlane rebuilt about 600 feet north of the intersection. This too burned in 1912. Still, the name lives on in today's "New Fairbank Hotel", now a popular night club.

Fairbanks' first church appeared in 1889 on the Vaughan Road. A few years later it was replaced by a new building on the southeast corner of Dufferin and Eglinton, and again in 1927

137

by the present red brick structure on the west side of Dufferin about one half mile north of Eglinton.

In 1888, the face of the area began to change. In that year, anticipating a suburban land boom, the Belt Line Railway promoters encircled the city with a commuter railway line. It crossed Dufferin north of Eglinton, where a station named Fairbanks was added. However, the economy collapsed and took the Belt Line with it. The land boom had to wait a few more years. Then, following the First World War, subdivisions began to appear on the farm fields, and a strip of stores started to fill in Eglinton Avenue. Today the intersection consists of stores, restaurants, banks and a newer church. Meanwhile, the original hamlet of Fairbanks has disappeared and lives on only in historical directories.

Dublin

Travellers continuing north from Fairbanks on the Gore and Vaughan Plank Road, eventually came to a toll gate at the intersection with what is today Sheppard Avenue. Farmers were just beginning to clear their land in the 1820s, and a hamlet sprang up by the toll gate. As usual, the early voyagers used the halt to partake of some refreshments, and to oblige them, William Duncan opened the Dublin House hotel on the northwest corner. Soon after, James Watson opened a small general store in the hotel, bartering with eggs, butter, and even cowhides. In 1854 he moved his operation to the southeast corner and acquired a post office with the name Carronbrook. That, however, was changed to Dublin in 1878.

The hamlet went on to add a school and a shoemaker, but little beyond that. Then in 1928 the DeHavilland Aircraft Company opened an airstrip, cutting off Sheppard Avenue west of the community. During World War Two, the air strip was enlarged to became a fullfledged military base, spawning housing and commercial development around it, and forcing Dufferin Street to veer around it to the east. In 1958, the Toronto Bypass, or the 401, was opened across the top of Toronto — "too far north" according to some of its critics —

nonetheless ushering in a suburban boom of backsplits and apartments. The boom never abated — the Yorkdale Mall, the Allen Expressway, and a subway extension, all arrived during the 1970s and 80s. Today traffic streams down Dufferin, swirling around the now closed air base, and onto the Allen. Dublin's days are long over.

Elia

Urging their teams further north along the Vaughan Road, the pioneer travellers came next to the intersection of Finch, and the hamlet called Elia. At the crossroads, John Gram operated a blacksmith shop at the northwest corner as early as 1837, while on the southeast corner William Troyer had added another by 1853. A little to the east, where the west branch of the Don River crossed Finch Avenue, John Willson operated a sawmill, while across the road, on the south side of Finch, William Wregget provided the farmers with a grist mill. A short distance north, Joseph James opened a water-powered sawmill which changed hands several times during its lifetime, ending up with Arthur Cowan in 1878. The mill sites lie now beneath the large flood control reservoir that forms the heart of G. Ross Lord Park, an extensive area of forested, rolling hills. Here yet stand a few scattered white pine trees that somehow escaped the teeth of the sawmill.

Prior to 1850, Vaughan Road was diverted well to the west to avoid the lowlands around the Don River. On this stretch, Jacob Kurtz operated a hotel with 15 rooms and 3 fireplaces. But when Vaughan Road was straightened, Kurtz relocated to the corner of Dufferin and Steeles, in a community then called Fisherville.

Elyah Church is Elia's only surviving structure.

139

Elia was a rural village, and not concentrated just at Finch and Dufferin. The post office, in fact, operated out of a general store a mile west at today's Finch and Keele. This building was built by Joseph Snider in 1878 and stood on the southwest corner. Previously, the mail had been delivered to a flag stop on the railway, halfway between the two crossroads, called York. However, as a few other places were using the name "York", the post office was called Elia. On the northeast corner, a school was opened in 1830, replaced in 1873 by a more substantial brick building. South of the store, the Canadian Order of Foresters added a hall which stood until 1956. Near the station, the Methodists built a church in 1832, replacing it in 1901 with a larger brick building.

But as with all these ancient crossroads hamlets, suburbia swept through, with widened intersections and new development removing all traces. The westerly intersection is now dominated by modern mini-malls, gas stations and donut shops while the farmlands between have become industrial. Surrounded by an oil company tank-farm, only the Elia church remains, about halfway between the two intersections, renamed "Elijah" Church.

Emery

Emery marked another one of those key crossroad intersections, this one, west of Elia, where Weston Road intersects Finch. Pennsylvania German settlers had made their way north along Weston Road, or at least the trail that preceded it, as early as 1799. M.S. Burkholder's general store was located on the northwest corner. Isaac Devins blacksmith shop and J.R. Devins carriage works stood on the southwest corner. In 1851 Frank Bunts was operating a shingle mill on a small tributary to the Humber River a short distance west, but 20 years later there was no record of it. North of the general store stood a community hall known as Canadian Home Circle Hall, while the local school houses stood on the northeast corner. At first the local mail was delivered to the blacksmith shop but after 1879, residents could pick it up at the store.

Usually when a railway comes to town, the place booms and prospers. That, however, was not the case with Emery. In 1870, the Toronto Grey and Bruce Railway laid their tracks across the community. The first station, called "Dayton", sat on the south side of Finch. Later, a new building was located west of Keele and called "Emery", to avoid confusion with another, somewhat larger railway centre, Dayton, Ohio. The station was only a shed-sized flag stop, and failed to turn the hamlet into the flourishing town that many had hoped. Although the building is long gone, some maps still show the name "Emery" by the tracks. The farms, too, are gone, replaced with industry, and the roads widened, passing now under the tracks. The only vestige of the little hamlet is the bell from the little red school house, preserved on the grounds of Emery Collegiate.

Emery's little flag station was removed many years ago.

Fisherville

Named after one of the many Pennsylvania German migrants to this area, Fisherville was the next hamlet that the traveller met while journeying northward from Elia on the Vaughan Road. It began to flourish around 1820 when Valentine Fisher built a sawmill. He later added a grist mill on the west branch of the Don River, east of Vaughan Road, where a few lots were created to provide houses for the mill workers. In 1855, when the Vaughan Road was straightened and planked, Jacob Kurtz opened a tavern to replace that which he had to close in Elia. The two-storey, wooden Fisherville Hotel stood on the south-east corner of Dufferin and Steeles. For half a century after-wards it was known as the "Cherry Inn" and ended its life in 1945 as the "Hanging Gate Inn". In that year, the University of Toronto demolished the structure to make room for its Connaught Medical Research Laboratory.

Fisherville's historic church is now in Black Creek Pioneer Village.

About the time that Kurtz opened his hotel, William Jackson erected a large house on the south side of Steeles, while a small Presbyterian church was added on the south east corner. Fisherville seemed to have more potential than most other little hamlets along the dirt road, but that optimism faded when the Ontario Huron and Simcoe Railway came through the area in 1853 and opened its Thornhill station at Concord, four kilometres to the northwest. New businesses opened by the station, and that community became the new focus for the rural area.

Today, Steeles and Dufferin is busier than it has ever been, but it is too late to save Fisherville. The buildings are gone, replaced by small plazas on both the southeast and southwest corners. The only survivors, and it's a surprise there are any at all, include Jackson's house, now part of a restaurant on the northeast corner, and the attractive little church, preserved in Black Creek Pioneer Village a short distance west.

Kaiserville

Now part of Black Creek Pioneer Village, Kaiserville consisted of a carpenter shop and wagon shop, both on Jacob Kaiser's lot, a sawmill on John Dalziel's farm, as well as a chapel and school. Of these buildings, none remain. However, the church cemetery and Dalziel's Pennsylvania-style farm buildings became the focus for the development of the pioneer village in the late 1950s. Since then, many historic hotels, houses, and stores have been hauled from as far away as Prince Edward County, making Black Creek Pioneer Village one of Ontario's most important heritage sites.

Downsview

It's a name that remains well known today, thanks to the presence of the Downsview Air Base. But in its heyday as a pioneer hamlet, it offered little more than a post office, blacksmith shop and school, all north of the intersection of today's Keele and Wilson. In fact, it had so little that one settler complained: "There is no store, post office or public building, only a church, and schoolhouse..." He lamented that "a tavern would pay well, as there is a great deal of traffic on our road". But, while a post office did open, named after the farm of John Perkins Bull, Downsview never did get its tavern or store.

It did however get a small shed-sized railway flag station on the Ontario Huron and Simcoe Railway, which, although it dropped mail and picked up passengers and milk, never attracted business. Most residents of the area found that the flourishing mill town of Weston was close enough to provide most of their needs: shopping, milling and drinking. Although surrounded by residential subdivisions, the church and the house that contained the post office still stand, both located at the

Downsview's church and one-time post office face each other on Keele Street at the corner of Tilbury.

143

The old Downsview flag station is only a memory, now.

corner of Keele and Tilbury. The house is now the Pet House Grooming Salon on the east side, while opposite stands the 1870 red brick church, with its graceful spire penetrating the sky.

Balmoral

Possibly buoyed by the arrival of the railway in 1853, John Sanford Fleming, inventor of Standard Time (for which he was knighted), tried his hand at land speculation, and in 1856 laid out a plan of subdivision which he called "Balmoral", advertising it as "a place where your children can play, with flowers and shrubs and shade trees of your own planting and fruits and vegetables of your own raising". But the idyll was too far away to tempt buyers, and the plan failed, the land remaining a farm in the Fleming family estate.

The Concord station as it appeared in the steam days. It was also called Thornhill station.

Concord

The Vaughan Road ultimately made its way into Vaughan township, and at today's Highway 7, spawned the hamlet of Concord. At first it was a typical crossroads settlement, with a general store, first opened by Peter Oster in 1846, a blacksmith shop opened by Isaac White in the same year, and a two-storey wagon shop. The post office opened in 1854 and was named for Concord Vermont, birthplace of Hiram White, an early resident. The community received a boost when the Ontario Simcoe and Huron Railway opened a station there in 1853. An attractive board-and-batten building with gracious, arching windows, it survived over a century before being demolished by CN in the 1970s. A sister station, originally in King City, now rests on the grounds of the King Township Museum.

Today, the intersection has been widened, removing all evidence of the early hamlet. Only two early buildings survive, both on the south side of Highway 7, east of the corner, and include a two-storey frame dwelling and a handsome, brick farm house which now contains Eagle Machining. Behind them, a subdivision has been added within the last 20 years.

145

Edgeley

Another Vaughan Township crossroads hamlet, Edgeley grew up at the intersection of today's Highway 7 and Jane Street. Here clustered a store, operated by J.H. Shank for a period of time, Peter Duck's hotel, plus a cider mill, a chopping mill, a church, a hall and a blacksmith shop. Nearby was James Hoover's wagon factory. A steam-operated shingle mill sat on the northwest corner, while the store stood on the southeast corner. Sam Snider's cider mill stood on the northeast corner, beside it was Garton's slaughter house. The hotel sat on the northeast corner but was turned into a residence before the turn of the century. The hall was built nearby in 1877 and was used primarily by the Independent Order of Good Templars.

There is no trace of Edgeley today. The widening of Highway 7 and Jane Street with their obligatory turning lanes, have left no room for history at this once busy pioneer intersection.

Woodhill

It wasn't known as Airport Road in those days, but simply as the Sixth Line. However, at the intersection of the Sixth Line with what is now Highway 7, there grew a little hamlet known as Woodhill. The place never had more than a church and a store with a post office, but the widening of the intersection has wiped everything away. The pioneer graves from the old cemetery have been encased in a common base, located south of the intersection on the east side of Airport Road, and, easy to miss from a passing car, are the only evidence of the hamlet's existence. Two other long-lost crossroads hamlets near Woodhill were Nortonville, halfway to Brampton, and Fraser's Corners, halfway between Nortonville and Mount Charles.

Grahamsville

Situated at the intersection of the Sixth Line and what was called Middle Road, now Steeles, Grahamsville grew into a sizable settlement. As with most, it started with a tavern, opened

146

by Thomas Graham in 1819. In the 1870s the Peel Atlas listed two churches, a store, post office and the Magnet hotel, built in 1831. On the northwest corner were Hempsey's blacksmith shop and John Watson's wagon factory, with his house beside it.

On the southwest corner stood Graham's general store, with its post office and dwelling unit, while south of that stood the short-lived Shiloh chapel, built in 1843 and demolished in the 1870s. On the northeast corner were William Wright's house and the Orange Lodge, while on the southeast corner stood the Masonic hall, the hotel with its 2 stories and 20 rooms, Peter Lamphier's general store, Maguire's shoe store, and the Anglican church. The hamlet was an important focal point for the entire community, hosting meetings and various community events such as agricultural fairs.

A fire in 1880 and another in 1882 destroyed a number of buildings including the blacksmith shop and a residence. But the thing that brought on Grahamsville's demise, as it did for so many of Ontario's little hamlets, was the arrival of the railway. The Grand Trunk laid its line well to the south, passing through Malton, rather than Grahamsville, and the place stagnated. Its population fell from a recorded high of 200 in 1864 to just 35 in 1908.

Grahamville's Magnet Hotel was destroyed by fire, the land now occupied by a gas station.

Following the Second World War, many of the old buildings lost their functions and, one by one, were demolished The last to go, in the late 1980s, was the historic residence located on the east side of Airport Road across from the cemetery. Now, gas stations and donut shops have invaded the intersection, and the only evidence of old Grahamsville is the cemetery.

Mount Charles

Leading west from Malton, the Derry Road carried many farmers to and from the mills at Meadowvale on the Credit River. As a result, a string of hamlets sprang up at many intersections. The first one west of Malton was known originally as King's Corners, after Charles King, an early settler. But when the post office opened in 1862, to avoid confusing the place with Kingsville in Southwestern Ontario, the hamlet took King's first name, Charles. Where the name "Mount" came from is unclear, as the whole area is flat.

By 1866 the corner could claim a pair of taverns, a sawmill and flour mill, as well as King's general store, and a blacksmith. In 1876, Robert McLeod was listed as the storekeeper and post-

This trio of buildings at Mount Charles provide an island of history in an endless ocean of industry.

master, as well as being an "architect". John Madigan was listed as an "innkeeper", although it was not likely at this intersection, and James Savage as a blacksmith. A church stood a short distance away, on the east side of Dixie Road.

The location today is under the flightpath of Pearson Airport's roaring jet airplanes, a constraint which keeps residential development at bay. However, the area is also part of an extensive industrial zone, one which stretches for several kilometres in all directions. Still, surviving in the midst of it all, is the brick blacksmith shop and the brick residence beside it. Hopefully heritage will prevail in this area, and these rustic pioneer structures will continue to tell the tale of the historic hamlet.

Palestine

The next stop west of Mount Charles was called Palestine. At the intersection stood a hotel, possibly Madigan's, a Methodist church and a schoolhouse. However, there was never a store or post office and the name did not long endure. Today it is part of the industrial and commercial area.

Derry West

Although the hamlet has vanished, this name lives on in the name of the road itself. One of the first places to locate here was the Derry West Hotel, described by a contemporary writer as a "good stopping place". The intersection also added a schoolhouse, a temperance hall, an Orange hall and a post office in the hotel run by Charles Armstrong. The name came from early settler James Brown, who dubbed it "Derry in the West", after his home, Londonderry, Ireland. None of the original structures survive. Several postwar rural homes were built in what was then still country, but by 1997, the bulldozers were preparing the ground for new developments.

Elmbank

Another busy farm road was the Britannia Road, again named

149

for its destination, the hamlet of Britannia. The first hamlet west of the Sixth Line (Airport road) was Elmbank. Named after the prestigious residence of John Grubb in the community of St. Andrews, well to the east (now Thistletown), it contained William MacKay's store and post office, Robert Spears' blacksmith shop, these on the southwest corner, while on the northwest corner stood a schoolhouse. A short distance south stood a Wesleyan Methodist church, while to the north there was a Catholic church.

The fate of this hamlet was decidedly unique. During the 1960s, in response to the demands of jet aircraft for longer runways, Malton airport expanded dramatically and Elmbank was expropriated for a new runway. Beneath the control tower of the airport, the trees and the foundations of this intersection sit undisturbed. A short distance north, close to the runway still lies the cemetery of the community. Pearson Airport is thus North America's only airport to have its own "ghost town." Britannia Road is fenced off at the airport boundary, and the only available glimpse of the old hamlet is from the seat of a jet.

Richview

A short distance south of Elmbank stood the hamlet of Richview. Long before Pearson Airport, or even Malton airport, for that matter, were conceived of, what is today Airport Road ran straight south from Malton, rather than bending east as it does today. The Sixth Line, as it was called, was only a farm road back then.

Here at the boundary of Toronto Gore and Toronto Townships, the little settlement claimed the usual crossroads compliment of post office, school, church and tavern. In 1888 the post office and the name were moved east to the third concession of Etobicoke and relocated in Watt's store at what was until then known as Kit's Corners. Here, at the intersection of "Richview Side Road", could also be found three blacksmiths, and taverns a short distance away at the fourth line, known as Ramage's Corners.

150

But the expansion of Pearson Airport removed all trace of the early version of Richview, while the suburban boom of the 1960s and 70s eliminated the later version. The Third Concession became Islington Avenue, and Richview Side Road became Eglinton Avenue. The only survivors are a pair of cemeteries. One, from the later location, stands on Martingrove Road, north of Eglinton, and is known as the Stonehouse cemetery; while the other, a relic of the orignal Richview, is familiar to travellers on the 427 as the little grave-yard that appears landlocked by Highways 427 and 401. However, it in fact lies on Eglinton Avenue which passes beneath the superhighways at that point.

Britannia

Here at the busy intersection of Britannia Road and Hurontario Street, a settlement road connecting Port Credit with Georgian Bay, grew the hamlet of Gardners Clearing, named after an early pioneer family. The hamlet grew to contain a post office, wagon factory, blacksmith, and, according to one early scribe, a "fine brick church." Fortunately, that fine brick church is still there, preserved and celebrated with a plaque. It was built in 1843, replacing a log church which had stood since 1830. The large pioneer cemetery stretches out behind it. Its appearance is incongruous, surrounded as it is by

Although the Britannia church has changed little since this photo was made 100 years ago, the foreground now contains a burger joint and six lanes of traffic.

151

a burger joint, donut shop and gas station, and subject to the roar of six lanes of traffic that now pass ceaselessly along Highway 10. Between Britannia and Elmbank, stood the rural community of Hanlon. It consisted of a rural population, a school, and a church on the southeast corner of Britannia Road and Dixie Road where the cemetery is the only survivor today.

Burnhamthorpe

Dixie Road, too, was a heavily travelled trail even in pioneer times, leading to the community of Dixie on the Dundas Highway. And so, at the intersection with Burhamthorpe Road, which led eastward to Islington Village, grew the hamlet of Burnhamthorpe with a church, store, blacksmith shop and wagon factory. A short distance away was the tavern and hamlet named "Puckey Huddle". Now surrounded by malls and apartments, only the church, on the northwest corner, remains.

Highfield

The roads which the early surveyors provided the farmers did not always do what the farmers wanted them to. That was the case with farmers in northern Etobicoke who wanted to get their grain to the mills on the Humber River. But the rigid grid of roads was too roundabout. To remedy this they petitioned the government to create what was called a "given" road, or one which cut across existing farm parcels. In 1833, the road, known as the Old Malton Road, opened and cut a swath from the northeast part of Etobicoke to the Fifth Concession Road.

At the corner of today's Martin Grove Road, a little hamlet grew up with the name Highfield. Here famers heading for the Humber could pause at Thomas Bailey's hotel, drop their horses off at Brooks' blacksmith shop, or visit the carpenter or the shoemaker. Another small nucleus of buildings clustered around the corner of today's Kipling as well. The church, known as the Sharon Church, was about a mile west on the Old Malton Road, while the school stood at the corner of Brown's

Line. The Grand Trunk Railway came through in 1856, and built a station it called Rexdale about a mile south. The name of the road was eventually changed to Rexdale Boulevard.

As suburbia swept through in the 1960s and 70s, the area became known as Rexdale, and was widened to four lanes, and industrial development wiped away the little hamlet. Today, nothing except the cemetery at the site of the Sharon church, and the little Rexdale station, which is now just a storage shed, have survived.

These topographic maps show how the old farm hamlets have vanished beneath seven decades of urban growth.

153

Barbertown

8.

⌒

By the Old Mill Stream

More important to Ontario's pioneers than even their roads, were their mills. Without their creaking mill wheels and grinding saws, there could be no flour and no lumber, vital for food and shelter. That many mills were built even before there were roads to get to them testified as to their importance. The few roads built in advance of the mills were key military routes like Yonge Street or Dundas Street, or highways like the Kingston Road. Weston Road, Islington, and Don Mills Road were exceptions making their way through dark forests to the mill sites.

Around the mills, settlements began to appear. Typically there would be the mill owners' homes, usually quite large, small cabins or boarding houses for the workers, if the mill was large enough, and a blacksmith or harness maker. Where the mills were likely to be around for a while (that is, on the larger rivers), the settlement would expand to include taverns, stores, churches and schools, and perhaps a townsite.

The Toronto area was luckier than most. The land was stone-free and fertile, and crossed by rivers; an ideal combination for a prosperous settlement to development. In the east were Duffins Creek, the Rouge River, and Highland Creek. Draining into the harbour was the Don River, with its two main branches. Defining the western boundary were the Humber River, Etobicoke Creek and then the Credit River.

Rising lake waters, which followed the retreat of the glaciers 50 thousand years ago, backed into the mouths of most of these streams to form little lagoons. These tiny harbours proved ideal for the development of schooner ports, from which farmers shipped their lumber or their barley to the booming American markets across the lake.

The valleys themselves, however, were steep and confined. And once the forests were cleared to make way for fields, no cooling cover remained to protect the water table. In spring, melting snow, rather than being absorbed into the soil, became raging flood waters which carried away mill dams, mills and sometimes entire mill towns. And in summer the streams evaporated, leaving the smaller creekbeds dry, and the mill wheels silent.

Big Valley, small river

The reason such a small river as the Don occupies such a large valley is due to the preglacial era when a river larger than today's Mississippi carved out a wide river valley.

Disastrous floods ravaged the ravines in the 1850s and 1870s, and again in the 1890s. Often the mills were built anew, but in other cases, there was no incentive to do so. Then in 1954, the worst storm in living memory, Hurricane Hazel, smashed away the last vestiges of a fading pioneer era.

The Rouge River

The Rouge River was described by William Smith in 1846, as a "good mill stream." And indeed many mills appeared along it, some very early on. It rises in two branches in northern Markham Township, with many water-power sites along its winding course. The settlers, brought into Markham Township by William Berczy in the 1790s, were attracted to the area in large part by the mill potential of the Rouge. Mills were built near the mouth of the river, where Kingston Road crossed it on a precarious wooden bridge (highlighted in the Kingston Road chapter). Others appeared at communities like Whitevale, a distinctive and historic community that has retained the flavour of its early mill days. Cedar Grove, and Markham village itself, are two other mill towns that have persisted, the latter the focus of much new development. Despite the development boom, Markham has retained its heritage townscape, as has Unionville, with its wonderfully preserved main street and residential districts.

Buttonville

The area around Buttonville was part of the early land grant given to Berczy for his settlers. In fact seven Berczy settlers were given farms along what is today Woodbine Avenue, or, as it was known then, the Fourth Line. By the 1830s the Baldwin family had a water-powered sawmill in operation on the south bank of the Rouge. In 1837, the Venice grist mill was added across from it. When the post office opened in 1851, it adopted the name Buttonville, after John Button, the first settler in the area. Although the place had been using the name "Millbrook" prior to that, another community by that name already had its post office, and the new name was chosen. By 1870, the village could claim three churches, three stores, the grist mill, and, a short distance south, a school.

Buttonville had hopes of being more than just a crossroads hamlet. In 1848, Button decided to subdivide part of his land into housing lots. Along with William Morrison, Button created a string of lots along Woodbine, with more laid out on back streets. Buoyed by Buttonville's optimism, new arrivals took up the village lots. More businesses arrived, including a blacksmith, a shoemaker, and a brickmaker.

Although Woodbine Avenue has changed from this dusty farm road into a wide suburban road, many of Buttonville's early buildings survive.

157

For a time, hopeful residents thought that they were onto an oil boom. In 1866, inspired by the success of the oil craze sweeping Southwestern Ontario, the Markham Oil and Mining Company began drilling for oil. But no black gold lay beneath the soils of Buttonville, and the company quietly folded.

The residents were disappointed yet again when the railways bypassed Buttonville in favour of Unionville to the east, and Richmond Hill to the west. By 1900 Buttonville had to content itself with being just another hamlet after all. The mills closed, the blacksmiths shut their doors, and Buttonville went to sleep. But it was shocked out of its dormancy in the 1950s with the opening of the Buttonville airport and the laying out of the Buttonville golf club. Suburbia had arrived. Throughout the 1970s and 80s the wave of housing and industry swept over the farmlands, accelerated by the opening of Highway 404 in the 1980s and the 407 in 1997.

One might have expected this tide of development to obliterate the historic community. Thankfully, that has not happened. In fact, much of the main portion of the hamlet still stands, although the back streets are potholed, traffic roars

This is the same view of Buttonville today.

158

past on Woodbine Avenue, now the mandatory four lanes wide, and much paint is peeling on the old wooden houses. But thanks to the pride that the residents of the Markham area show in their heritage, the old structures have resisted the 20th and perhaps will resist even the 21st century.

On the east side of Woodbine, coming south from 16th Avenue, there is the Bliss House, built in 1860 by wagonmaker James Bliss, the Burr farmhouse, which dates from 1875, the "Little Antique House", built around 1853, the Thomson store dating from 1860, the 1850 Padgett house, and John Craig's brick house, built in 1875. On the back street are a pair of houses, one dating from 1859, the other from 1870.

Along the west side are the foundations of Robert Baldwin's mills, while on the north side of the bridge is the Baker House, built in 1845 (Buttonville's oldest), the cobbler's houses, built around 1850, and the 1851 store that housed Buttonville's post office. Three early buildings sit on the narrow backstreet behind these buildings.

But perhaps the village's best preserved building is the little schoolhouse. Perched on the south end of the village, SS #5 educated children for nearly a century in true pioneer fashion. After sitting as a maintenance facility for several years, it was bought by a developer and moved a short distance away to become a schoolhouse museum, managed by the York Region Board of Education. Like the rest of the community, it gives modern residents an opportunity to glimpse an era that most could scarcely imagine.

Headford

A short distance upstream huddled the tiny mill village of Headford. Here, where the Rouge crosses today's Leslie Street, a short distance south of Major MacKenzie Drive, John Burr and Frederick Eckardt opened saw and grist mills. Built in 1832, the Burr mill, tiny at first, passed through a succession of owners, growing and expanding with each one. In 1861, John Eyer bought it and added a woollen mill; in 1889 someone named Hislop altered it into a roller mill. But with the growth of the

159

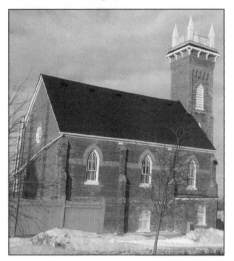

The Headford church remains a hilltop landmark, despite being surrounded by a sea of surburbia.

prairies, Ontario mills were losing their competitive edge. By 1912, the Headford operation had become a simple chopping mill, and in 1916, four years after a dam break, it was demolished.

Although the community never kept pace with Buttonville, it did acquire a church, known as Leeks Chapel, James Wellman's store, William Teasdel's black smithshop, and a number of other village trades. By 1880, an estimated 175 people lived there. It, too, was the site of oil drilling during the 1860s, but, as in Buttonville, all wells came up dry.

Development finally spread into the fields around Headford during the 1990s, leaving only a couple of the village's early vestiges. Leading east from Leslie, south of Major MacKenzie, a private lane traces the old street that led down to the mill. Here yet stands a stone house built around 1834 by Christian Hendricks. The most visible reminder of this pioneer mill village, however, perches prominently on a hill just south of that — the Headford United Church. With its tall spire visible for many miles around, it has been an area landmark since 1882, when it was built to replace the earlier chapel.

The Don River

Although it is the Toronto area's best known river, it is also the smallest, with lesser flows than those found in the Rouge, Humber or Credit. Rising in the vicinities of Maple and Richmond Hill, the Don meanders southward in two branches which meet where Don Mills Road today crosses the Don Valley Parkway. Although small, the river attracted several early saw and grist mills. Few, however, became the focus for anything more than a scattered rural settlement or hamlet. Then, following the disastrous flooding of 1878, many communities were simply left derelict.

Todmorden Mills

In 1793, soon after Governor Simcoe had selected "York" as his new capital, the Skinner brothers, Isaiah and Aaron, built what were the Toronto area's first saw and grist mills on the banks of the Don in the vicinity of today's Pottery Road. The operations were subsequently run by Parshall Terry, and, after his tragic death by drowning, by Thomas Skinner who lost his life in the War of 1812. During this period, they were known as the Don Mills.

In the 1820s, two families arrived in the region from Niagara-on-the-Lake. They included John Eastwood and his father-in-law, Thomas Helliwell. On the site of the Skinner and Terry mills, they set about creating one of Toronto's first industrial empires. They started with a brewery, then when the government announced a contest to start the province's first paper mill operation, they converted the grist mill to a paper mill and went head-to-head with one James Crooks of Ancaster. Crooks won by a scant two days. But that didn't deter the Helliwells and a visitor in 1833 remarked upon the "... beautiful and verdant flats (where) are situated the York Paper mills, distillery and grist mill of Messrs. Eastwood and Co., and Messrs. Helliwell's large and extensive brewery". The Helliwells and Eastwoods themselves referred to the place as "Todmorden Mills", after their home in Yorkshire.

The Helliwell house is preserved today in Todmorden Mills historic park.

The Road to the mill at first followed Winchester Street from Parliament Street, winding into the Don Valley where the Toronto Necropolis sits today. A large beech

161

tree used to lie across the river as a bridge for this road. Today's Danforth ramp to the Don Valley Parkway represents the historic route's alignment up the east wall of the valley. Later, the road was opened from Queen Street, where a better bridge crossed the river, and followed today's Broadview Avenue to Pottery Road which led to the mills. At that time, the mills were known as the Don Mills, and Broadview Ave as "Don Mills Road".

Then, in the 1840s, the empire changed hands. Following the death of Thomas Helliwell in 1825, his son Joseph carried on until 1847 when fire struck, severely damaging the Helliwell home, the brewery and the paper mill. In 1855, three brothers, John, Thomas and George Taylor, took over the operations. The Lower Mills, as they were called, comprised the paper mill and brewery. The Middle Mills made up the York Paper Mill, and at the forks of the Don, where Don Mills Road today crosses the river and the Don Valley Parkway, were the Upper Mills. All three became the Taylor Paper Mills. After fire damaged the Lower Mills in 1900, they were taken over by Robert Davies who ran the operation as part of his enormous industrial empire

Todmorden Mills was built partly because of a contest set up by the local government of the day. John Eastwood and Thomas Helliwell lost the prize to James Crook, who completed the construction of his settlement only 48 hours before the last brick was laid at Todmorden.

until 1928. The Middle Mills became part of the Howard Smith Paper Mills in 1939, later Domtar, which demolished the buildings in the early 1990s. You can still visit the old foundations and chimney in a vacant lot beside the Don Valley Parkway.

The remains of the brewery hall, the paper mill, the Parshall Terry house (1798), and the Helliwell house, (1837) have become the focus of the Todmorden Mills historic park. The little turreted railway station that sat below the Queen Street bridge was later moved to the site, and today the park sponsors community events and houses the East York archives. The only other sign of the Don Valley's industrial heritage is the brickyards, which stand on the north side of the Bayview Extension, west of Pottery Road, and is the subject of a preservation campaign.

Oriole

It's hard to describe exactly where Oriole really was. Most histories put it at or near the intersection of Leslie and Sheppard Avenue, in the southern reaches of North York. Its many mills, however, were scattered along the branches of the Don River, each branch over several kilometres. The earliest operation was that of William Marsh who erected a sawmill in 1814 near what is today the 401, a little east of Leslie Street. But it was short-lived, being washed away in a flood in 1818. The mill site remained quiet until 1846 when Michael Shepard reactivated the mill. His brother Thomas added a grist mill a decade later. After the mills burned in 1869, a sawmill continued to function here until 1878.

Other than the mills, all that Oriole could offer was a church and a blacksmith.

The railways did arrive at Oriole, but too late to make a difference. When the Canadian Northern decided to built through here in 1904, the mill era on the Don had ended, and urban growth was beginning to break free of Toronto's bounds a short distance south. Originally called Duncan, the Oriole Station stood south of York Mills Road and east of Leslie. Despite efforts to preserve it, the station was demolished in 1988.

A handful of early buildings at the site of Gray Mills are the only mill buildings left in the Don Mills area.

Today the area has been so altered that it has become a challenge to visualize a landscape where forests covered the gentle slopes of the valley, and little, wooden mills creaked beside the rushing waters. Now, the intersection of Leslie and Sheppard is a constant flow of cars turning and roaring along in six lanes of traffic. The North York general hospital stands on the southwest corner, luxurious housing sprawls on the slopes on the north and southeast corners, while the valley of the Don stretches away on the northwest corner. West of the hospital, a dead-end street known as "Old Leslie Street" follows the road's original route, although it offers no historic structures.

Further from the intersection a couple of houses survive from those early days. On the south side of Sheppard, between Leslie and Bayview, Thomas Clark in 1841 began farming the land, and in 1855 constructed a large, brick house. Today, surrounded by evergreens, the house, with its fieldstone foundation, brick floors and two chimneys, looks decidedly out of place amid the shopping plazas and housing developments that now occupy his fields.

Meanwhile, east of Leslie Street, former Ontario premier George Henry built a massive brick house overlooking the gentle valley in 1898. It stands on George Henry Boulevard, but is

164

best viewed in a more natural setting from the park in the valley to the south. A cairn located a little further west on the road was erected in tribute to Henry and Jane Mullholland, who pioneered the area in 1806, a time when the forests were thick, and no mills existed.

Flynntown

A series of sawmills operated on the Don a little south of Finch Avenue between 1822 and 1885, and briefly a little south of that between 1850 and 1860. The latter area also went by the name of Flynntown, after a shoemaker named James Flynn. This little community could also claim a blacksmith, a store, a school and a church, all near the intersection of Leslie and Finch. The mills had long vanished by the time the century turned, likely washed away in the floods of 1878, while the blacksmith and store lasted a while longer. The school and church, however, still stand, the latter preserved beside an apartment and shopping centre east of Don Mills Road, the former a schoolhouse museum on the south side of Finch between Don Mills Road and Leslie.

Don Mills

Farmers north of the Don River were anxious to improve their roads, and in 1825 donated land to open a previously unsurveyed road they called the Don Independent Road. At first it extended south only to the river, but by 1852 it was built across the valley to meet Plains Road, now O'Connor, and became part of Don Mills Road. At that time, "Don Mills Road" also referred to Broadview, and O'Connor.

But the community of Don Mills was considered to centre around the intersection of the Don Independent Road and Lawrence Avenue. Here a store stood on the northwest corner, a school on the southeast. Most of the mill activity occurred in what is today Wilket Creek Park, at Leslie and Eglinton (although neither road existed in that location at the time) where four sawmills briefly operated during the 1850s and 60s.

165

However, the larger mills were found north of the intersection. Among the earliest were the saw and grist mills of the Gray brothers, William and Alexander, built in the 1820s. A little further south was the little sawmill operated by Smith Humphrey, although it lasted only until the 1870s. Another was that of Alexander Milne who, in 1827, opened a saw and woollen mill on Wilket Creek, a tributary of the Don, in what is now the lovely, landscaped Edwards Gardens. Because of low water flow even then, Milne would later move his operation to the main branch of the Don. Milneford Mills sprang up next to it. Nearby, on the southeast corner of Don Mills Road and Lawrence, there stood a little red school house, on the northwest, a tavern operated at various times by John Elliott and John Carruthers. A half mile north of the intersection were a blacksmith and store with a post office.

Many of the mills were damaged or destroyed by the raging flood waters which swept down the valley in 1878, and most milling in Don Mills ceased at that time. Only the Gray grist mill kept on churning until 1914 when the property was sold to mining magnate David Dunlap, who converted the property into a summer estate. The large Gray house still stands at the southeast corner of Don Mills Road and Legato, while at the end of the mill road, now a private lane leading to the Donalda Club, are another pair of the Grays' early houses, along with a portion of the mill which was incorporated into a magnificent barn.

Milnesford Mills

Here, where the Don Valley Parkway passes beneath Lawrence Avenue, was the only real mill village to develop on this stretch of the Don River. In 1832 Alexander Milne moved his mills here from the site of what is now Edwards Gardens because of the low flow there. In 1846 he built a new woollen mill and by 1861 was turning out 2,000 yards of cloth a year, and 400,000 feet of lumber. But the devastating floods of 1878 swept away his entire village. Rather than give up, Milne's sons, William and Alexander W, decided to rebuild.

This time they built one of the most magnificent mills on

166

While the solid old brick mill (top) is long gone, the frame house (bottom) near the intersection of Lawrence Avenue and the Don Valley Parkway is Milnesford Mills' only survivor.

the entire Don. The new brick woollen mill stood three stories high, and measured 80 feet by 50. It rested on a stone foundation, capped with a mansard roof and graceful cupola. Here, too, they converted William's first house into housing for the workers, and added a large new home for themselves. Although the mill closed in the early 1900s it was demolished only in 1946, in order to recycle the bricks.

Fires and floods took their toll, but the final coup was Hurricane Hazel in 1954. Now a widened Lawrence Avenue has replaced the dirt track which once twisted through the valley. And all evidence of the mill village lies beneath the six lanes of the Don Valley Parkway. The only survivor is one of the Milne houses, sitting on the east side of the valley on Old Lawrence Avenue, now part of the new Sauriol park.

167

German Mills

Yonge Street had not even been surveyed when William Berczy brought nearly 300 Pennsylvania German settlers into the forested wilds of Ontario. Most were given land grants in Markham Township, where many of their descendants yet live. A small group, however, opted to create a small village on the banks of the Don a short distance east of the village of Thornhill. Here they built a sawmill, flour mill, distillery, and blacksmith shop as well a number of small, drafty cabins, their only shelter against the bitter winters. By 1805 Berczy was busy trying to convince the government to build a canal along the Rouge River to the Markham area, where his other followers were settling in. Although he did clear and partially construct a portion of it, he became embroiled in a financial dispute with the government, and put German Mills up for sale. In his book Toronto of Old, Dr. Henry Scadding described them as "an impressive sight... in the middle of the woods.. their windows boarded up". German Mills had become Ontario's first ghost town.

While the buildings quickly disappeared, the mill dam remained evident until the 1970s. Today, John Street follows

A sign on John Street in Thornhill commemorates one of the Toronto area's first lost villages, German Mills. It was a ghost town by the 1820s.

the alignment of the old road from Yonge Street to the settlement, which originally ended at German Mills Road. German Mills Road leads into the valley from Don Mills Road now, passing one of the Toronto area's more attractive pioneer relics, the old board-and-batten German Mills community hall. Built somewhat later, in 1843, it still survives on a large lot shaded by trees that were around when the area was still farmland. Now lined with luxury homes, German Mills Road dead-ends and becomes a pathway into the ravine, where a plaque recounts the story of this ill-fated settlement.

The Humber

Flowing wide and swift, the Humber became one of Toronto area's most important mill streams, at one time counting more than 80 mills of various sizes and types. Its headwaters begin in the scenic Oak Ridges Moraine between Nobleton and King City, and were once the site of "Toronto Carrying Place", a native portage that linked Lake Ontario with Lake Simcoe. For a time Governor Simcoe contemplated building a portage road along the banks of the river, but instead chose a straighter route further east, now known as Yonge Street.

Milton Mills

Many in Toronto are familiar with the long-established Old Mill Restaurant. The name "old mill" dates back to the very beginning of settlement in the area. To help encourage settlement, the government of the day financed the construction of saw and grist mills. One of Ontario's earliest was known as the King's Mill, built by the government in 1794 to supply the first settlers with lumber to build their homes and barns. Around the mill, later operated by John Gamble, grew a village, now long forgotten, with the name Milton Mills, with workers' cabins, a blacksmith, cooper, wagonmaker, and of course the Milton House tavern. On the hill to the west of the mill stood Gamble's large home, while in the river in front of the mill were the barges that were able to navigate upstream from the

169

lake. In 1848 Gamble's mill burned and was replaced by a towering stone building. In 1881 it too burned and its stone shell became a popular ruin for nearby city dwellers to explore. To take advantage of the idyllic surroundings, Robert Home Smith in 1914 developed the lands around the valley, and opened the Old Mill tea room.

Today, the area has changed little. The tea room has now become a restaurant widely known for its rustic atmosphere and fine dining. The haunting ruins nearby remain a popular destination for photographers and heritage enthusiasts. As for the village itself, all that might have remained has been washed away by a succession of floods and changes to the river.

Brownsville

In 1830, John Brown arrived in a mill village named Burwick, on the banks of the Humber north of the busy mill town of Weston. Here he built a mill and dam, which became the focus for a little community of mill workers called Brownsville. By the late 1800s three mills were busy creaking away on the side of the river, while a street led from Weston Road to the river bank.

By 1877 the Brown interest had been taken over by the Wallace Brothers, a name which continued until 1923. Today all evidence of early Brownsville has gone. Burwick became known as Woodbridge, absorbing Brownsville in the 1880s. The mill road now leads to the legion hall, while a small plaza and carwash have obliterated the village site at the southwest corner of what is today Highway 7 and Islington.

Pine Grove

Pine Grove today is a residential neighbourhood in Woodbridge. But 150 years ago, it was one of the Toronto area's leading mill towns. Here, where the rushing waters of the Humber wind through a wide and flat valley, John Schmidt settled the area and opened a grist mill. In 1840 John Gamble moved from the King's Mill on the lower Humber and bought out

170

Smith's operation. With his eyes firmly set on expansion, Gamble realized that the Toronto area was a growing market, and he added woollen mills and a brewery.

Then in 1860 the giant Gooderham and Worts firm of Toronto bought out Gamble and added a distillery to the operation. By the time Pine Grove's 200 citizens were celebrating confederation in 1867, their town could count, besides the industries, a general store, three hotels (the Commercial, the Pine Grove, and the Cameron), churches and a blacksmith, as well as other businesses typical of a small Ontario village. Then in 1935, the Hayhoe family bought the mill business from the Hicks family and operate it to this day, the last mill to function on the Humber. During their stewardship, the mill has exported to England, Russia and China, among other countries.

It doesn't use water power any more. In fact, one of the old grind stones sits in front of the front door to the company office. Fate was not as gentle to the rest of the early village buildings. Most of those left standing after the spring floods of the 1800s were destroyed by the wind and rain that thundered down from Hurricane Hazel in 1954. There are a few, however,

Pine Grove's one-time main street, is today a quiet lane in the booming community of Woodbridge.

171

which did survive. The mill itself, on Pine Grove Road east of Islington, is updated, and bears no resemblance to earlier incarnations. Beside it, the old company store still stands, and nearby, the last of the 1870s residences. Another early house stands at the northwest corner of Pine Grove and Islington, while one of the old hotels lingers on, now as a home, near the southeast corner of that same intersection.

Pine Grove Road was once the village thoroughfare, but when the river washed away the bridge, that route was severed and only a pedestrian bridge now crosses the water. On the east bank, a town plot was laid out in the 1800s, although only a few lots were taken up. Today, however, these village lots, on their traditional grid network of streets, contain new monster homes, more typical of sprawling suburbs than of an old mill town. Similarly, newer houses and businesses also line Islington Avenue through what is today the heart of the community. But were it not for a historical marker at the south end of the old village, it would be hard to know where Woodbridge ends and Pine Grove begins.

The Credit River

The longest of the Rivers that flow into Lake Ontario's west end, the Credit, begins its course in the vicinity of Orangeville, tumbling in two branches which meet in the spectacular Forks of the Credit gorge. Several busy and ever-growing towns owe their existence to this river — Alton, Inglewood, Georgetown, and Streetsville. However, some of the Credit River's offspring fared less well, and now number among the many lost mill villages of the Toronto area.

Barbertown

Streetsville is a town that is proud of its history, and has done its best to preserve its old main street. That has been no mean feat given the pressures exerted by urban development, where the bottom line leaves little room for history. But even within this oasis of history, one historical village has all but vanished.

William Barber's mansion is now a popular Streetsville restaurant.

In the early 1820s, following the survey of Toronto Township, John Beatty led a colony of Irish settlers up the valley of the Credit. In response to the needs of the pioneers, mills were built at several water-power sites, giving rise to places like Streetsville, Churchville, and Meadowvale.

In 1830 William Comfort built a grist mill on the banks of the Credit River, just south of a mill erected a decade before by Timothy Street. In 1843 the site was acquired by the Barber Brothers who added a woollen mill. As early as 1837, the Barbers had mill operations in Georgetown, but needed more room, and the open banks of the swift Credit gave them just that. By this time settlers were filling up the farmlands, and creating a market for the growing numbers of mills along the Credit River. In 1852 the Barbers merged the two operations at Streetsville.

The brothers were no strangers to the business. The foursome had come from Ireland straight to Crooks Hollow where, in what was then Ontario's leading industrial centre, they learned the many miseries of milling. By 1837 they were ready to create their own industrial empire and chose Georgetown as

173

a place in which to start. But Streetsville is where they ended up. Here, more than a mile from the Street mill, and the town that was springing up beside it, the Barbers went about building a town of their own. They provided 43 dwellings, each with a small plot of land, and boarding houses for their workforce of nearly 200. Besides the mill, they also operated a two-storey general store , with dry goods, groceries, and boots. Under the management of Mr. J.G. Owens, the six employees were doing a brisk $50,000 a year.

The woollen mill itself was lit by gas manufactured on site, and measured 125 feet by 50 feet and stood four stories high, churning out 900 yards of tweed a day, worth $120,000 a year. The Barbers' brother-in-law, Bennet Franklin, operated a sawmill, Barney McCusker a blacksmith shop, and R.A. Redding a tailor shop with up to 15 seamstresses. The community was a social centre as well, with dances rocking the rafters of the boarding house on Saturday nights, while those who preferred their recreation under the sun could play cricket on the flats beside the mill.

This is not one of those mill stories that ends with the mill burning down. Rather, the Barbers' empire faltered in 1884, and the mill operated only intermittently for many years after. Gradually the town became deserted, considered by many to be a ghost town. The store sat empty, the wool house became a residence, and most of the workers' homes were demolished. But, as in Pine Grove, the mill is still there, today operated as the Adam Milling Company. But much has changed. Gone is the water power, and most of the 43 houses. The river valley, much flooded, and swept clean of its earlier structures, is now a private recreation area. Suburbia has crept over the hills, and look-alike houses stretch as far as the eye can see. The old Barbertown Road is no longer open to through traffic, and the bridge over the Credit is restricted to pedestrians. The mill itself has been much altered and enlarged. But the one-time store still stands as a house, near the west side of the mill, while the lovely brick mansion built by William Barber has become a restaurant and stands prominently at the northeast corner of

174

Barbertown Road and Queen Street, Streetsville's main thoroughfare.

South of the mill, where the severed portion of Barbertown Road meets Eglinton Avenue, a pair of workers' duplexes have received new siding and now house a day care.

Churchville

The sign that announces the scattered houses in the quiet valley says "Churchville, ca 1815". which makes it one of the Credit Valley's oldest mill towns. Indeed, by the late 1840s, it was described as "one of the most flourishing villages in the county". Here with 150 inhabitants, it contained one grist mill, two sawmills, two blacksmiths, two wagonmakers, and a Methodist chapel, as well as "factories of different kinds". John Atchison operated the North American Hotel, while Thomas Clifford and J.E. and R. Pointer provided general stores. The town was laid out on a network of streets on both shores of the river.

But the railways arrived and passed the place by. The Grand Trunk went through Brampton instead, four miles to the north, and Churchville stagnated. Even the arrival of the Credit Valley Railway in 1873 did nothing to help the place recover, and by 1880 it was down to just "a couple of small stores and a good hotel", according to a contemporary observer.

And today, the community looks pretty much the same. A few original buildings line the main drag, including one of the old stores, and on the rim of the valley, the hotel. But there are no churches on Church Street, and no mills on the river, although the millrace remains visible. Instead there is a pleasant riverside park. Although being in a flood plain, where new development is now restricted, a few newer houses have appeared on some of the old village lots. But up on the farm fields that surround the site, the bulldozers were, by the late 1990s, poised to engulf Churchville with more of the monotonous and unstoppable urban sprawl. It is likely that some vestiges of the village will linger on.

Meadowvale

By contrast, the struggle to preserve historic Meadowvale has been markedly more successful. Here in 1831, James Crawford and John Simspon got the place going with two sawmills and a carding mill. Being on the busy Derry Road, more businesses began to locate here and the mill village added stores, taverns and churches. In 1844 Francis Silverthorn arrived and expanded Crawford's mills to include a grist mill. In 1857, the ever-growing Gooderham and Worts firm took over the Silverthorne mills, operating them until 1880. The grist mill continued to grind out flour until 1950 and four years later was demolished.

But Meadowvale did not die with it. Rather, it has survived as one of Ontario's heritage success stories. Although only about two dozen buildings still linger on, they, in the 1980s, became Ontario's first heritage district. Through grants and loans then available to home owners, the buildings have been preserved, and a walk through the community is like a stroll into an era that time has forgotten.

The community sits just west of Second Line West on Old Derry Road. By the river, the remains of the old mill can still

The historic Meadowvale District is still one of Ontario's best preserved heritage areas.

Much of historic Meadowvale village remains intact, including Charles Gooderham's old mansion.

be seen, while between the river and Second Line, a string of early buildings gives the place its 19th-century aura. These include, on the north side, the Commercial Hotel which dates from 1852, now an apartment building. Beside it is the Hill House, built in 1840, and on the northeast corner of the Second Line, set on a large, treed property, the 1870s Gooderham mansion, built for Charles Gooderham. Following the departure of Gooderham in 1880s, the house served variously as a summer resort, a private dwelling, and more lately as apartments.

On the south side of Derry Road are the United Church, built in 1863, the Graham Pearson House, a red brick residence built in 1870, the two-storey brick general store, a relative newcomer dating only from 1916, although a number of earlier stores were operated by Silverthorne and the Gooderhams. Separated from the store by a more modern gas station stands George Ball's 1844 hotel. A number of delightful smaller houses dot the back lanes of Mill Street, Pond Street and Barberry Lane, including a one-time boarding house for Silverthorne's mill workers, and a pair of mill workers' duplexes. Heritage Mississauga includes the historic district on one of their informative and attractive walking-tour brochures.

Today the name "Meadowvale" is more commonly applied to a massive suburban development of shopping centres, and endless acres of suburban housing, although newer houses are attempting to replicate the 19th-century styles of the old mill town. But in the midst of it all, like an oasis, the real "Meadowvale" remains a true piece of the past.

Rowntree Mills

Near today's intersection of Islington avenue and Finch, the Humber River flows close to the road. This, in 1843, was where Joseph Rowntree realized there was enough water power for the mills he intended to build. On the west bank, opposite Rowntree's mills, William Kaiting was operating a sawmill and grist mill, turning them over to Henry Boulton in 1851, who in turn passed them on to Rowntree's son, James. Nearby, where Finch itself crosses the Humber, William Crosson ran a sawmill from 1848 until at least 1860. Just north of Finch and Islington, on a small tributary of the Humber, John Duncan also operated a small sawmill. But by the 1860s, the supply of timber was becoming depleted, and sawmills were shutting down.

Much of this lumber was used to construct the Pine Ridge Methodist church which stood on Islington, just north of today's intersection with Rowntree Mills Road in 1845. The original mill road was a short distance north.

Rowntree Mills never really became a village. Rather, it consisted of various mills, a couple of inns and a church. Farmers hauling their loads to and from the mills usually had time for a bit of refreshment, and the taverns on Islington catered well to that need. Edward Phillips' "Plank Road Inn", situated in a small log house, stood south of Islington and Steeles, while William Mackay's inn stood on the northwest corner of that intersection.

Little evidence of early Rowntree Mills has survived. The area became a popular summer resort area known as Humber

Summit, after the mill era ended, but even that was largely washed away in the raging torrent of Hurricane Hazel. Rowntree Mills Road leads west from Islington Avenue down to the river where a wide, grassy park covers the riverbank. Rowntree's large home stood until 1965, then a restaurant, when it burned. Only the street name, and the cemetery that marks the site of the old church, tell the early story of this once busy Humber River mill community.

Scarborough Village

9.

ᘒ

The Railway Towns

The final form of distinctive community to develop was the railway town. Even as the new fangled horseless carriages were clattering down dusty roads, the railways remained the only reliable year- round transportation for both passengers and freight. When the railways first arrived, everything changed. Little crossroads hamlets, once the social and business centres of rural Ontario, suddenly became backwaters, doomed to stagnate. Factories replaced the village artisan, and the station became the new focus for the community.

The railway also ushered in new towns and villages. There were several different kinds of railway villages. Most common were the station villages. New communities were laid out, usually in a standard grid plan, and usually just behind the station, where a hotel, stores and houses, all attracted by the station, were built. By the station itself stood the water tower, coaling dock, and warehouses. Where there were key railway functions, special villages were created to cater to them. These might be railway junctions, yard facilities, or an atypical role, such as a helper-engine yard. By contrast, some railway points spawned nothing in the way of village growth. These were the little railway flag stops, sheds where milk cans were picked up, mail dropped off, and where passengers stood shivering in the tiny sheds that bore the station name.

Although the all consuming role of yesteryear's railways is little remembered, passengers on VIA Rail or commuters on GO transit realize that, as they watch the traffic jams, or the paralysing blizzards from their warm coaches, rail remains the superior way to travel.

Mimico

Until it amalgamated with Etobicoke, Mimico had been remembered as a modern west end Toronto suburb, a role it still plays. Traffic roars along its main streets, Lakeshore Boulevard, Royal York Road and the Queensway, hurrying to and from the commercial development that lines them, and the suburban sprawl that fills in the space between them. But when it was a distinct village, far from the urban sea that would ultimately engulf it, Mimico was a small railway town.

The name Mimico has been around a bit. An Indian name for the "home of the passenger pigeon", it was first given to that portion of Lambton Mills that stood along Dundas Street on the west side of the Humber River. Development at the mouth of the Humber was originally related to the hotels that clustered by the Lakeshore Road toll ferry, later a bridge, and the mill village known as Milton Mills. Church Street (now Royal York Road) was later opened to link the area's two main roads, Dundas and Lakeshore.

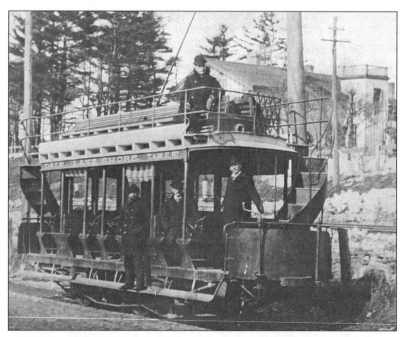

One of the early streetcars that served the Mimico area.

TORONTO - MIMICO RAILWAY YMCA

The railway YMCA provided home away from home for railway crews stopping over at the Mimico yards.

In 1853, the railway construction crews began to lay down the steel rails for what was originally called the Hamilton and Toronto Railway, in effect a branch of the Great Western Railway, to link Toronto with its main line at Hamilton. The first station, a simple, wooden structure, was located on the north side of the tracks, at the foot of today's Windsor Street. Then, with the building of the Windsor Hotel on the south side, the station was relocated there. Later, when the Grand Trunk opened its New Toronto yards, it built yet another station on the north side of the tracks, but west of Royal York Road, behind which the YMCA added one of its much lauded railway Y's. Between 1856 and 1860, a model workers' community was laid out south of the tracks between Church and Burlington Street. But the workers were unable to afford the long commute into the Toronto factory area, and the planned community remained only sparsely settled.

Gradually, the little grid network of streets began to fill and Mimico became a typical station village, with the hotel and the railway operations located along Manchester Street, and the shops and churches along Mimico Avenue. By the turn of the

183

century, the changes that would engulf the little railside village were beginning to appear. The nearby lakeshore was becoming hot property for wealthy Torontonians looking for a cool lakeside retreat from the city's steamy and smoky summer air. Street railway service began to Port Credit in 1892, and by 1906 was being operated by the Toronto and York Railway Company, bringing with it a land boom along the Lakeshore Road. In that year, an even more profound change occurred. The Grand Trunk opened its sorting yard a short distance west in a new community called New Toronto. Now pinched by growth from both east and west, Mimico became part of a burgeoning urban area, and lost its rural distinctiveness. The opening of the Hamilton Highway in 1916, and the Queen Elizabeth Way in 1939, both hastened the process of urbanization.

Today's wider roads, highway commercial plazas, and endless housing have made it even harder to locate "old" Mimico, but parts are still there. The heart of old Mimico lies northwest of Lakeshore Boulevard, where Albert and Superior Streets lead north to Cavell. Here, near the corner of Cavell and Station Road, a few old early workers' homes mix with newer-style dwellings. A few blocks south, along the railway village's commercial core, old stores still line Mimico Avenue, but only

a couple have retained any commercial function. A pair of early churches stand near Royal York, which subsequently developed into the community's busiest intersection. The old hotel still stands too, now known as the King George, located on Manchester across from the tracks. The most recent of Mimico's stations also still stands, although just barely, on the west side of Royal York Road, north of the tracks.

The old Grand Trunk station in Mimico is still standing – but not for long.

184

New Toronto

Like Mimico, New Toronto was a product of the railway. Unlike Mimico, it was a major planned town, and arrived on the scene relatively late in the game. By 1890, the lakeshore area west of Toronto was beginning to fill in. To the west lay the summer playground of Long Branch, to the east Mimico. Then in 1890, the Globe carried a prominent story, entitled grandly: "Toronto's Growing Suburb, New Toronto". New Toronto was more than just a new suburb; it was a whole new town. Centred around today's Islington and Lakeshore, New Toronto was laid out in 1891 in a grid of numbered streets leading north and south of Lakeshore.

In 1893 the electric street-railway cars began clanging into the new town, and soon after came the industries: Pease Furniture, Brown's Brass Rolling Mill, Menzie's Wallpaper Plant, and, during the height of the First World War, the Goodyear Tire and Rubber plant in 1917. Other major industries included Campbells Soup, and Ananconda Brass and Steel. But the backbone of New Toronto's industry was the massive sorting yards established there in 1904 by the Grand Trunk Railway. Here they created maintenance facilities, a roundhouse, repair shops and housing for the workers.

While the town plan extended to 32nd Street, the core of the community was in the 5th, 6th and 7th Street areas, and between New Toronto Street on the north and Lakeshore on the south. In 1913 the community had gained a population large enough to earn it incorporation as a village, and by 1920 as a town. Lakeshore Boulevard

The New Toronto repair shops were busy in the days of steam. Today they are a fading memory.

185

(then called the Hamilton Highway) had become lined with stores, and the old village core was no longer distinguishable. The land south of Lakeshore Boulevard, once home to a handful of summer cottages, was subdivided and filled with houses.

The Queen Elizabeth Way was opened in 1939 and, during the 1950s and 60s, brought a vast industrial park north of the tracks, as well as more houses and malls. Islington Avenue was extended over the railyards on a modern four-lane bridge, severing Seventh Street removing many early structures. In 1965 CN relocated their sorting yards to Brampton, and when VIA Rail, as well as GO Transit later moved in, they saved few of the old CN yard buildings. Finally, in 1967, New Toronto lost even its incorporated status to join Etobicoke as one of Metro Toronto's six municipalities.

Still, there are many parts of the old village that can be seen. The older commercial buildings are still evident at the corner of Lakeshore and what is now Islington — the art deco former post office, opened in 1936, on the northeast corner, and the original stores now occupied by Ben's Hairstyling and TNT Footwear on the northwest. Examples of early workers housing line Fifth Street between Birmingham and the Lakeshore, Sixth Street as far as New Toronto Street, and the portion of Seventh Street left as a dead end by the extension of Islington Avenue, a cul-de-sac now called Toffey Court. Near the Lakeshore, a number of newer houses and stores have replaced several of the older buildings that once stood on Seventh Street, now Islington. At the intersection of Kipling and Lakeshore, at the west end of the village, the former Almont Hotel still stands.

Most of the industries and railway buildings are gone as well. The roundhouse, coal tipples and yard office which stood on the north side of New Toronto Street, between Seventh and Kipling, are now only rubble. At Kipling and New Toronto Streets are the only structures to date from the railway operations, and include a brickyard office and an old boxcar converted to a maintenance shed. Most of the historic Goodyear plant was demolished, amid considerable controversy, for a condominium development. Only a small portion survives on

186

Birmingham Street. Most of the remaining industries have been reduced to vast fields of rubble except for a few old-buildings on the northwest corner of Birmingham and Islington. A former company office is now the Heritage Soups restaurant at the northwest corner of Lakeshore and Eighth, a few paces north of the handsome fire hall.

But the most significant heritage structures in New Toronto predate the village itself. These are the buildings that make up the complex known formerly as the Lakeshore Psychiatric Hospital (originally the Mimico Lunatic Asylum). Built in 1888 to ease overcrowding in the Queen Street Asylum, the complex of buildings, in a quiet country setting, was deemed preferable to the impersonal institution on Queen Street. Although decommissioned a decade ago, the buildings still stand, magnificent examples of institutional architecture of the period. Having been declared to be of provincial heritage significance, a designation almost unheard of in Ontario, they now form part of the Humber College campus, as does the century old Cumberland House nearby. These spectacular buildings sprawl in a park-like setting beside the lake south of Lakeshore Boulevard and east of Kipling.

The Cumberland House near Lake Ontario in New Toronto.

187

West Toronto

It may be difficult to convince longtime residents of West Toronto, or "The Junction" as it is more commonly known, that theirs is a "lost" village. In many ways, it is not. Many of the streets, the houses, and even residents themselves, still survive from the time when West Toronto Junction was a noisy and bustling railway centre. But, although many trains still rumble through, they no longer stop, and the facilities and jobs that they spawned are gone.

Before the railways, the area was a quiet country place, of trees and half-cleared farms scattered along a dusty wagon track known grandly as the Dundas Highway. A hotel and toll gate stood where Dundas crossed what is now Bloor, beyond which stretched the extensive holdings of one John Scarlett, with his estate house known as Runnymede.

But the peace and quiet would not last, for the rail era was about to arrive. The first railway to cross through the area was the Grand Trunk, in 1856, which erected the Carlton station where the tracks crossed St. Clair Avenue. Then followed the Toronto Grey and Bruce in 1873. Its line was laid down immediately beside that of the GT, and the area began to boom. Then in 1879 when the Credit Valley Railway used this location as a junction for its line west to Galt, the name "junction" came into use. The fourth and final line arrived in 1883, when the Ontario and Quebec Railway completed its Toronto bypass from the east, and West Toronto Junction became a major railway junction.

All this activity attracted the attention of a land speculator named Daniel Clendenan, who bought up the 82-acre Carlton Race Course which, along with other acquisitions, allowed him to register a townsite of 240 acres. Consisting of two dozen city blocks, most of it lay west of Keele and south of Dundas. In a little over a year he had sold 170 lots, the price doubling and nearly tripling in price during that time. By 1888, West Toronto had enough residents to become incorporated as a village, and a year later, as a town.

The hub of activity was the intersection of Dundas and

188

Keele. Here were the three-storey Campbell Block, the White Swan Hotel, and a hardware store belonging to a town councillor named Peake. Several businesses began to appear along the south side of Dundas, among them Fisher's store, the J.B. Bruce block of stores, Wylie's drug store, and Shaw's fuel operation. The first CP station was located in the diamond of the junction at Dundas and Weston Road. So great was the land boom that 26 real estate offices were soon operating along Dundas, demanding $500 per foot for commercial land that just two years earlier had been going for one tenth that. In the first year alone more than 600 houses were built, complete with sidewalks and water mains

As in many railway towns, the industries soon began to arrive as well.Among the first were Dodge Pulley Company, Canada Wire Mattress, and the prestigious Heintzman Piano Company. As might also be expected, the town became a rowdy assemblage of railway and factory workers, most of them anxious to put a hard day of work behind them in the local pub, and West Toronto soon had six. However, the boozing was not without its detractors, who were eloquent enough to push through, in 1904, a local option bylaw which made West Toronto dry, one of the Toronto's area's last wards to remain so.

Churches, libraries and schools all made the community one of the Toronto area's most complete railway towns. New stations were built; that by the Grand Trunk in 1890 closer to Weston Road, and that by the CPR in 1911 to the south of the original station. The latter was an attractive Tudor style station, a storey and a half high, and with a long shelter extending the length of the platform to the south.

In 1908, the town was annexed to the City of Toronto, and lost its status as a separate municipality. Following the arrival of the Toronto Suburban Railway in 1898, and the electric streetcars soon afterward, Dundas Street had by the 1920s developed into a continuous commercial strip, dominated by utilitarian storefronts of indifferent design. The community had become part of Toronto not just politically, but physically as well.

Although West Toronto may have lost its physical separateness, it has never lost its community identity. Still known as The Junction, it has retained pride in its heritage, and in its early buildings, several of which still stand. The Campbell Block (1901) still dominates the northwest corner of Keele and Dundas. Three stories high with arched third floor windows, it stretches a considerable distance along Dundas. Unfortunately, its grandeur is diminished by peeling paint and unsympathetic facades on the several small ground-floor stores. The Thompson building at the southeast corner (1890) has over the years housed architect James Ellis, the Toronto Suburban Railway, Bell Telephone and the Sterling Bank, and today is home to the Concourse Restaurant. A short distance east, the unimposing Simcoe Block, built in 1886, represents the oldest commercial building still standing on Dundas.

The Heintzman house in West Toronto is a reminder of the community's railway boom years.

Annette Street, the town's residential thoroughfare, although wide and busy, is dominated by church steeples and grand houses such as Theodore Heintzman's palatial "Birches" (1890) at Laws Street, and George Edgar's 1887 Queen-Anne-style villa at Annette and Evelyn. The earliest of the workers' houses line the side streets closer to Dundas Street.

Sadly, many key structures are gone. The old post office and town hall which once stood on the southwest corner of Keele and Dundas were removed and replaced with a parking lot. The historic Peacock Hotel which marked the pre-rail intersection of Dundas and Weston Road has been gone for a half century, the site marked now by a donut shop. Perhaps the strangest demolition was the removal of the Old Weston Road bridge. Built in 1911, it

190

had deteriorated to the point it could no longer safely carry traffic and in 1972 it was closed, and demolished a decade later. The abutments yet stand, as do the approaches, a bizarre and unappreciated monument to early road engineering.

But the most controversial and tragic demolition of them all was that of the CPR's West Toronto station. Despite heroic attempts by local heritage enthusiasts and the City of Toronto to save the building, CPR's then president, Ian Sinclair, rejected plans to recycle the beautiful station and during the night of November, 1982, ordered in a wrecking crew. By dawn the depot was dust. The public outrage which followed this outburst of corporate vandalism reverberated across the country with profound repercussions. While the City charged the CPR with illegal demolition, the federal government enacted special legislation designed to designate and preserve railway stations. When that legislation was presented to the Senate, the only senator to vote against it was the newly appointed and unrepentant former CPR president, Sinclair. To date more than 150 have been designated across Canada, many of them belonging to a chastised CPR.

In 1994, another neglected station was struck when the abandoned Grand Trunk station on Weston Road, north of The Junction, was gutted by fire. Although its brick shell remains solid, its future does not.

East Toronto

By 1883 the Grand Trunk, spurred into action by the building of the National Dream, the CPR, had begun to assemble an empire of its own, gobbling up the many little resource lines that crossed Southern Ontario like a spider web. To accommodate its booming traffic, it needed new sorting yards east of Union Station. The only extensive area of land that was both flat and still cheap lay well to the east, roughly where a crude wagon road called Dawes Road crossed their main line to Montreal.

Here the Grand Trunk built a sorting yard, and a townsite grew up beside it. Surrounded by farm fields and market gar-

The site of East Toronto's "York" station is now occupied by a glass GO train shelter.

dens, the town of East Toronto was laid out between Danforth Avenue and Kingston Road, and between Victoria Park and Main Street. Here were seven miles of sidings, enough to store 420 cars, and a 32-stall roundhouse. A long, low station, built in the Grand Trunk's style of the late 19th century, and called York, was added on the north side of the tracks, immediately east of the new bridge that spanned Main Street. Dawes Road was closed and its southern stretch between the tracks and Kingston Road was absorbed into the yards and the townsite.

Main Street became the commercial core of the village — hence the name — with businesses lining the road south of the tracks and around the Gerrard intersection. Here, W. H. Snell opened a bakery on the southwest corner, a building large enough to contain an auditorium upstairs. Opposite, on the southeast corner, H. Snell operated a grocery store with a tailorshop beside it. At the northeast corner stood the stately railway YMCA (relocated there in 1903 from its 1891 location on the south side of Gerrard) as part of that organization's efforts to improve the deplorable working conditions faced by trains crews. Along Main between Swanwick and Gerrard, and along the north side of Gerrard east of Hannaford, stood a string of railway workers' housing.

A number of early industries were located along the tracks,

192

including Rogerson Coal at the southeast corner of Osborne and Gerrard, another coal yard north of the tracks beside Main, and the McMillim and Costain lumber and planing mill beside the Main Street bridge east of Norwood Terrace.

On the west side of Main, by the foot of the bridge, were Taylor's cigar shop, the Ideal Theatre and the Ulster Temple which witnessed dances and wrestling matches alike. By 1888, East Toronto had a population large enough to incorporate as a village, and in 1903, as a town. The council met first in the upstairs of the fire hall, then in a town hall located at Swanwick and Main. Those chambers weren't needed for long as the little railway town was absorbed by the growing City of Toronto just five years later.

The community still remained "in the country" at that time. But during the 1920s, development began to follow the street-cars along Gerrard and Danforth, and the city's urban fringe moved in, surrounding East Toronto and filling in the vacant village lots.

Despite some new growth in the area, little has changed in and around East Toronto since then. A new police station was built on the site of the town hall in 1910, and still stands, now used as a community facility. The fire hall beside it, built around the same time, also remains in use. Railway workers' houses still line Gerrard and Swanwick between Main and Kimberley. Another line of early houses marks the north side of Stephenson Avenue (named after the village's first reeve) between Main and Westlake. The McMillim and Costain block of stores still dominate the southeast and southwest corners of the old Gerrard, and Main intersection, while several of the old industries have been recycled into new uses along the north side of Gerrard east of Main.

Much, however, has gone. The magnificent YMCA was torn down in 1930 and replaced with the Ted Reeve arena which stands today, although the field behind it is still known as the Grand Trunk Fields. The station, too, was removed in the 1960s, in its place a GO station, although the old station platform can still be identified. The CN yards still see occasional

193

use, although most of the rails, and remaining structures were removed in 1997. Many of the businesses that lined Main have been replaced by more current operations such as Vince Parrell's Dance Centre, while the coal yard on the corner of Danforth and Main is now the site of highrise apartments.

Scarborough Junction

Scarborough Junction was in fact two junctions. From the time the Danforth Road was opened through the area in the 1790s, it formed the junction of that pioneer path with two busy farm roads, Kennedy Road, and St. Clair Avenue, where the farm hamlet of Bell's Corners flourished. However, the name "Junction" appeared only after the second junction was formed, that of two railway lines.

In 1856, the Grand Trunk opened its route connecting Toronto with Montreal. At that time the village was little more than a flag stop on the busy line. But in 1873, another railway line appeared on the scene. This was the Toronto and Nipissing Railway, anxious to add a route northeast of Toronto to tap into the resource potential of the region known as the Kawarthas. The route followed the Grand Trunk from Toronto, using narrow-gauge line at first, to Scarborough Junction. Here it branched northward, building at the junction a large station. The depot adopted the two-storey pattern that it used in other larger centres along the line, like Kirkfield, Victoria Road, and Coboconk. The lower portion of the station consisted of a freight shed and waiting room for the passengers, while upstairs the agent enjoyed his living quarters of three bedrooms.

Because of the new functions, the land to the west of the new line was laid out into a village, using the typical railway grid pattern of streets. The main streets in the village were Linden and Laurel, both of which ran parallel to the TNR between St. Clair and Danforth Road. Several new buildings appeared along St. Clair immediately west of the crossing and included a church, Baines' blacksmith shop and a row of workers' houses. Here too was the widely known Everest Store. Built

194

Scarborough Junction's handsome station burned in 1958.

in 1906, after having previously occupied the former Bell General Store at St. Clair and Kennedy, it became one of the most prosperous general stores in the township, and the building lasted into the 1970s.

The 1950s suburban boom swept through the area about the same time as the TNR was shutting down. In 1965, the TNR, by then under the ownership of CN, ran its last train to Coboconk, and over the succeeding years, the rail was lifted between there and Uxbridge. With the growth of suburbia in northern Scarborough, the southern portion of the line retained a commuter service, now operated by GO as far as Stouffville. From Stouffville to Uxbridge, the York and Durham Heritage Railway operates excursion trains using historic passenger coaches and a 1950s era diesel engine. The handsome Scarborough Junction station burned in 1958, replaced today by a GO station on the south side of St. Clair.

While much of Scarborough Junction survived the onslaught of the 1960s suburban growth, it did not survive the 80s. In 1976, a deadly crash between a TTC bus and a train prompted politicians to install a much-needed grade separation. To make way for the underpass approach and road-widening, the old St. Clair Avenue buildings had to be removed. The Baines blacksmith shop and the Everest Store at St. Clair and Linden were among those removed to allow for the construction of the underpass, and the site of the store is now an ambulance station. Although new houses filled in the vacant lots along Laurel and Linden, a few of the old Junction homes stand out among them. These include the Vivian, Walton, and Graves buildings at 48, 41 and 23 Laurel respectively, and the Trinnel house at Harmony and Magnolia.

Scarborough Village

This was one of those many speculative railway towns. When railways arrived, land owners dreamed of reaping wonderful profits from subdividing their land into a thriving town. It was a dream that only occasionally came true, but that didn't stop Isaac Stoner. In 1856 the Grand Trunk built its line through Scarborough, detouring around a difficult series of hills which stood in the way of their lakeshore alignment. Engines were required to puff up a steep grade and then around the hill before regaining a downward gradient. At the height of the grade and at the apex of the curve, the railway crossed Markham Road, already a busy farm road. Here Stoner laid out a town plan on 40 acres, selling lots by auction for $428 per quarter acre.

The town included a store, blacksmith, school, and Baird's Hotel, but only about a dozen houses. Because of the steepness of both the grade and the curve, the railway found stopping and restarting at the station to be difficult and relocated their station about a mile west near the Midland Avenue crossing (where Scarborough Junction would later grow). Whenever stops were required at Scarborough village, the trains would use the hotel, but it ceased to be a regular station stop. In fact, by 1896, Scarborough Village was considered by many to be a ghost town and most of the lots remained empty.

Suburban growth occurred in the area in two phases. During the 1960s, most of the farmland around Scarborough

196

was subdivided for houses, and the empty lots in Scarborough Village filled in. Markham Road was widened and a new bridge was built over the railway. During this wave the historic hotel and the other structures which lined the west side of Markham Road vanished. Through the 1980s, growth intensified, and with it came the widening of Eglinton to six lanes and the construction of condominiums and commercial plazas. What remained of Scarborough Village along Eglinton fell during this onslaught.

The only way to trace old Scarborough Village now is to follow the main road of Stoner's plan, Centre Street, north from Eglinton. On Centre, a short distance north of Eglinton, stands the old Washington Methodist Church manse, built in 1875, and now occupied by the New Life Tabernacle. A smaller village cabin also stands on Centre Street closer to the tracks. North of the tracks, a road called Bakerton follows Stoner's plan beside the tracks, bending north briefly along the Centre Street alignment where another old village house has survived. Otherwise, the housing north of the line dates from the 1970s while that south of it dates from the suburban boom of the 1960s.

Port Union

Despite its name, the main purpose of Port Union's existence was not the lake, but the railway. During the 1840s, farmers from the townships of Pickering and Scarborough would bring their produce to the wharf for shipment across the lake. But because the location was right on the township boundary, no one could agree on a name, and Port Union was adopted as a compromise. But being utterly exposed to the wind and the waves, the port did not develop into a settlement.

That had to wait until 1856, and the arrival of the Grand Trunk Railway, whose route followed the lakeshore wherever possible. But in this vicinity, steep gradients both to the east towards Rosebank, and to the west, proved too much for the smaller early steam engines. Port Union was ideally situated for a small yard where the railway could store helper engines —

197

locomotives that would provide the extra power needed to haul the trains up those hills.

A small townsite was laid out and consisted of a station, a water tower, the yards, and hotels operated by Will Hetherington and Thomas Laskey. Eventually, with the arrival of larger steam engines, and then diesels, the helper yard was no longer needed. Finally the station itself closed in 1967 and was demolished. Soon afterward, suburbia arrived. Housing filled the fields north of the tracks, while Johns Manville opened a large factory to the west. A short distance east of the old station grounds, GO Transit has built a new commuter station, and the location sees more trains now than at any time in the past.

Located at the end of Port Union Road, south of an extended and widened Lawrence Avenue, old Port Union hasn't benefitted from the boom. On the streets once lined with railway houses, only two remain, while the old Laksey Hotel stands boarded and vandalized. The sidings that once held the helper engines are barely visible through the tall grasses beside today's busy line. Until the last vestiges of its railway heritage are finally gone, Port Union will stand as a ghost town of Toronto's railway era.

Leaside

Like East Toronto, New Toronto and West Toronto, Leaside is not particularly "lost". The fact that it was conceived of and created by a railway company that few today have even heard of, is. Named after the farm home of William Lea, an eight-sided estate house that burned in 1913, Leaside is the only town in Southern Ontario to have been completely planned by a railway company.

Latecomers to the railway building scene, William Mackenzie and Donald Mann were still trying to complete their Canadian Northern Railway at a time when the CPR was 25 years old, and the Grand Trunk had been around for a half century. In 1912, as part of their Ottawa main line, they needed a place for yards and maintenance facilities. And, having successfully created the towns of Port Mann British Columbia, and Mount Royal Park, in Quebec, they were anxious to reap more riches in Ontario. Here, near the property of William Lea, north of the tracks laid down by the CPR's Ontario and Quebec Railway in the 1880s, the two intrepid railway men asked their town planner, Frederick Todd, to repeat his magic and lay out what would be the Town of Leaside.

Between Bayview and Laird Avenue, Todd designed an appealing plan with a commercial area, a town centre and curving streets, many named after Canadian Northern Railway dignitaries, like Thornton, Hanna, Wicksteed, Laird — and Canora, an acronym of Canadian Northern Railway. In September of 1913, the lots in the 1000-acre townsite went on sale, and Leaside became an incorporated town.

East of Laird, a vast tract of land was set aside for industry. The first to locate was Canada Wire and Cable. With a contract to provide shells to the army for the First World War, the company needed new terrain for their munitions plant. Leaside, with its newly completed plan, and vacant industrial land, was ideal, and in 1914 work began on the massive complex. Adjacent to the factory the government added one of Canada's first airfields. Again, thanks to the newly created industrial site, and level terrain, Leaside proved perfect and by 1917 the nine hangars were complete. With the war over, the airstrip became the site of Canada's first airmail flight when Captain Brian Peck brought 120 letters from Montreal in June of 1918.

In 1967, Leaside amalgamated with the Township of East York and lost its separate municipal status. It has never, however, lost its community identity, and, like West Toronto, remains a distinctive Toronto neighbourhood. Nor has it lost much from its early days as a railway town. The curving streets retain their handsome brick homes, while the old town centre, on McCrae between Laird and Millwood, with its tennis courts, library and former town hall, remains a focus for the community. Although the industrial area was drastically enlarged during the 1960s and 70s, a few of the early industries yet linger. A portion of the Canada Wire and Cable plant still stands at

Wicksteed and Laird, although unfortunately the last of the historic airport hangars was demolished in 1971.

A pair of the Canadian Northern's railway buildings have managed to survive the area's redevelopment. The yards and station were situated east of Laird, where Esandar now runs, and here, on the south side, sits the former yard station, and on the north, the engine repair shop, while the rusting sidings are overgrown behind a fence. In contrast, the CPR line immediately beside it is still in use, and is one of that railway's busiest lines.

The Lost Stations

The Toronto area was once a hub of railway lines. Dozens of trains per hour shuffled along the tracks stopping at the stations to pick up or deposit passengers. During the first decade of the 20th century, this area could claim nearly 80 railway stations. Of that number only a dozen still stand today. While most of the larger villages and towns that dotted the lines counted sizable combination freight and passenger stations, many isolated little flag stations flourished briefly and then vanished, forgotten by all but a few.

The Canadian Northern Railway could claim stations at Todmorden, the junction of its eastern line to Ottawa and its northern line to the Canadian West. It stood a little east of the site of today's Leaside bridge, with another at Duncan, near today's York Mills Road. Both were two storey wooden depots, the former having been demolished for decades, the latter lingering long enough to become the subject of a failed preservation effort, while Thornhill was apparently served by a station on John Street called Thornlea. Small railway settlements grew up around both Duncan and Thornlea.

The CPR, which assumed the Toronto Grey and Bruce, the Ontario and Quebec (OC), and the Credit Valley railways, had stations on the OQ line at places like Donlands, where the CPR crosses over Don Mills Road, Brown's Corners, Agincourt and Leaside. Others stood on the former CVR line at Lambton, Dixie, Cooksville and Streetsville. More were located on the TGB line at Weston, Emery, and Woodbridge, with the famed

200

The Credit Valley Railway's (later the CPR's) old Lambton depot is but one of the Toronto area's many lost stations.

junction station at West Toronto, and a flag station at Carlton.

The Grand Trunk, however, could claim the lion's share of station locations. Steaming east from Union Station, the Grand Trunk's passengers could look out their windows at the Riverdale station at Queen Street, the York station at Main, as well as others at Scarborough Junction, Port Union, Rosebank, Dunbarton and Pickering. On its westbound trains, gazers could look out on stations at the CNE, Sunnyside, Mimico, Long Branch, Port Credit, Clarkson, Lorne Park, Oakville, Bronte and Burlington, all on the former Great Western line. Those following the former Grand Trunk line to the northwest would pass stations at Parkdale, West Toronto, Rexdale, and Malton, and north along the Northern line at St. Clair, Downsview, York, and Concord. The ill-fated Belt Line had stops at Rosedale, in the Don Valley, at Moore Park, Yonge Street, Eglinton, and Fairbanks.

Railway stations were vital in the days of dusty roads, and slow horse-drawn transportation. Everything and everybody travelled by train. The stations were where families greeted long-lost loved ones, or said a sobbing farewell to sons and hus-

201

bands, heading off to war, not knowing if they would ever see them again. However, with the arrival of cars, and more modern railway technology, the depots became redundant, and during the 1950s and 60s the Toronto area lost nearly all its remaining stations. A handful still cling to life at Mimico, West Toronto, Rexdale, and Leaside, although just barely, for none fulfill any useful function. The CPR's elegant North Toronto depot will be restored as part of a development project in the vicinity. However, only Toronto's acclaimed Union Station retains both its grandeur and its trains. Incredibly, during the 1970s, it too was destined for demolition. And it is threatened once again, with the proposal to build a new Maple Leaf Gardens on the site.

Acknowledgements

My thanks go to those many dedicated local archivists, historians and librarians who shared with me not just their valuable research and resources but the love of their local history. Without these elements this book would not have happened.

Index

Recommended Reading

And a Mill Shall Be Built Thereon, East York Historical Society, 1996
Carleton and Davenport Revisited, A Walking Tour, West Toronto Junction Historical Society
Footpaths to Freeways, the Story of Ontario's Roads, Ontario Ministry of Transportation, 1984
Golden Years of East York, Borough of East York, 1976
Heritage Tours of Erindale, Streetsville, Cooksville, Meadowvale, Heritage Missisauga
History of Scarborough, Robert R. Bonis, Scarborough Public Library, 1965
Historical Walking Tour of Todmorden, East York Historical Society,
Historical Cycling Tour of Little York, East York Historical Society
North York, The Pioneer Years, North York Historical Society
Remembering the Don, Amethyst Press, 1981
Scarborough Then and Now, City of Scarborough, 1996
Town of Leaside, A Brief History, East York Historical Society
Walking Tour of Islington, Etobicoke Historical Board
Walking Tour of Pickering Village, Pickering LACAC
Waterfront Trail, Waterfront Regeneration Trust, 1995
West Toronto Junction Revisited, West Toronto Junction Historical Society, 1992

Photo Credits

p. 1   City of Toronto Archives (James 1094)
p. 12   Metropolitan Toronto Reference Library (T11513)
p. 13   Metropolitan Toronto Reference Library (MTL 1149)
p. 24   Metropolitan Toronto Reference Library (MTL 1842)
p. 36   City of Toronto Archives (SC 246-2)
p. 42   Metropolitan Toronto Reference Library (T11089)
p. 45   Metropolitan Toronto Reference Library (T11008)
p. 46   Metropolitan Toronto Reference Library (T12525)
p. 51   National Archives of Canada (PA 179542)
p. 57   Metropolitan Toronto Reference Library (SI-1084)
p. 61   Metropolitan Toronto Reference Library
p. 67   City of Toronto Archives (James 7277)
p. 68   Metropolitan Toronto Reference Library (978-13-6)
p. 80   Metropolitan Toronto Reference Library (T12535)
p. 83   Metropolitan Toronto Reference Library (T30048)
p. 96   City of Toronto Archives (James 1093)
p.144   Dick George
p.145   D. McCartney
p.185   Metropolitan Toronto Reference Library (SI-3391B)
p.190   Metropolitan Toronto Reference Library (T-12196)
p.195   Len Appleyard
p.201   CP Archives (A-21040)

backcover: Dick George

all other photos by Ron Brown